Ordination of Women to the Diaconate in the Eastern Churches

Essays by Cipriano Vagaggini

Edited by Phyllis Zagano

A Michael Glazier Book

LITURGICAL PRESS
Collegeville, Minnesota

www.litpress.org

Please note that the pieces here were originally published as follows:

Cipriano Vagaggini, "Le diaconesse nella tradizione greca e bizantina," *Il Regno* 32 (1987) 672–673. Cipriano Vagaggini, "L'ordinazione delle diaconesse nella tradizione greca e bizantina," *Orientalia christiana periodica* 40 (1974) 146–189.

A Michael Glazier Book published by Liturgical Press

Cover design by Ann Blattner. Image: Hemera/Thinkstock by Getty Images.

Library of Congress Control Number: 2013955711

ISBN: 978-0-8146-8310-1   978-0-8146-8335-4 (e-book)

Contents

Introduction

The question of restoring women to the ordained diaconate surfaced during the Second Vatican Council and continued to resound in academic and pastoral circles well after Pope Paul VI restored the diaconate as a permanent state for the church in the West in 1967. The diaconate has continued uninterrupted in Eastern churches since apostolic times.

In 1974, Cipriano Vagaggini, OSB. Cam. (1909–1999), published "L'ordinazione delle diaconesse nella tradizione greca e bizantina," in *Orientalia christiana periodica*, a publication of the Pontifical Oriental Institute under the editorial direction of Robert F. Taft, SJ. Vagaggini, at the time a member of the International Theological Commission (ITC), reportedly wrote the 15,000-word work at the request of Pope Paul VI, who had asked about the possibility of admitting women to the ordained diaconate.[1] Vagaggini responded in the affirmative.

Vagaggini's research into the historical details of women ordained as deacons in the Greek and Byzantine traditions demonstrates that women were actually ordained to the major order of deacon over the course of many centuries in many parts of

[1] Cipriano Vagaggini, "L'ordinazione delle diaconesse nella tradizione greca e bizantina," *Orientalia christiana periodica* 40 (1974): 146–89. See Peter Hebblethwaite, *Paul VI: The First Modern Pope* (New York and Mahwah, NJ: Paulist Press, 1993), 640, regarding the possibility that Vagaggini's article is actually a suppressed study of the International Theological Commission.

the Greek and Byzantine East. In his *Orientalia* article, Vagaggini carefully reviews the liturgies used to ordain women, which are substantially the same as those used to ordain men, and assays the commentaries contemporaneous to women's ordinations to and exercise of the diaconate.

Vagaggini introduces the conclusions to his study by noting that "in Christian antiquity there were different beliefs and tendencies distinguishing between ministry and ministry, ordination and ordination, with regard to the nature and significance of the respective orders or ranks." These conditions noted, he presents seven points:

1. *The Apostolic Tradition* of Hippolytus (c. 210) does not mention "deaconesses" but clearly includes those who serve as deacons in the group comprising bishops, priests, and deacons, who receive the laying on of hands, as opposed to lectors and subdeacons, who did not. Hippolytus adds as a general principal: "*cheirotonia* is given only to the cleric (χλῆρος) in view of the λειτουργία" (the service focused on the altar). The Western tradition after Hippolytus distinguishes the two groups based on the laying on of hands and later including the *traditio instrumentorum* or the anointing.

2. On the other hand, the Eastern tradition had many ordinations. Therefore, the distinction between the "orders" is not made on the basis of the laying on of hands. Byzantine euchologies distinguish between *cheirotonia* and *cheirothesia* in the eighth century and following; after about the middle of the twelfth century apparently only the presbyter and deacon are ordained by *cheirotonia*, whereas lower ministers would be ordained by *cheirothesia*, a simple blessing. Nonetheless, the ancient Greek tradition established a distinction among groups of ministers: bishop, presbyter, deacon, deaconess, lector, subdeacon.

3. Epiphanius of Salamis distinguished the ministers who belong to the ἱερωσύνη—bishops, presbyters, deacons, subdeacons—from those who do not belong to and only come *after* the ἱερωσύνη: lectors, deaconesses, exorcists, interpreters, under-

takers, and doorkeepers. But it is uncertain what Epiphanius meant by ἱερωσύνη, or why, for example, the subdeacon belongs to it but the deaconess and the lector do not.

4. Theodore of Mopsuestia witnesses an ecclesiastical law disallowing ordinations of lectors at the foot of the altar inside the sanctuary because "they were established subsequently," "they do not minister the same mystery," and, therefore, "they are instead outside of the ranks of Church ministry." Theodore is a witness to the theological belief of distinction between the bishop, presbyter, deacon group and the lector, subdeacon group. Theodore understands deaconesses to be an apostolic institution, and, since the *Apostolic Constitutions* attest to the ordinations of deaconesses in the presence of the presbytery, it appears these ordinations occur in public in front of the altar in the sanctuary.

5. In the Byzantine tradition of euchologies from the seventh to the fourteenth centuries, deaconesses always seem to have been ordained at the foot of the altar inside the sanctuary in contrast to the ritual for the ordination of lectors, subdeacons, or other "offices." Other details for the Byzantine ordination of deaconesses go along the same lines. It seems certain to Vagaggini that, in the history of the undivided church, the Byzantine tradition maintained that deaconesses belonged to the group of bishops, presbyters, and deacons.

6. Given the above, Vagaggini concludes that theologically, by virtue of the use of the Byzantine Church, it appears that women can receive diaconal ordination, which by nature and dignity is equated to the ordination of the deacons.

7. Vagaggini affirms that the liturgical work of the deaconesses was more restricted than that of the male deacons, a now obsolete fact regarding distribution of Communion and many other tasks since by indult women do almost everything the clergy can except say Mass, hear confessions, and anoint the sick. It is also true that the ancient tradition of the church unanimously denied women the possibility of entering the priesthood.

Vagaggini's article and especially his conclusions gained notoriety in scholarly circles. In the ensuing years, two liturgy scholars, Roger Gryson and Aimé-Georges Martimort (1911–2000), wrote competing works about women in the diaconate. Gryson's *The Ministry of Women in the Early Church* finds that women were ordained to and ministered within the order of deacons. In *Deaconesses: An Historical Study*, Martimort profoundly disagrees with both Gryson and Vagaggini[2] and calls Vagaggini's *Orientalia* article a "seductive presentation of the case" (for ordaining women as deacons).[3]

Discussion and academic debate about women in the diaconate continued, in many quarters overshadowed or conjoined with discussion and debate about ordaining women as priests. Such led (and still leads) to confusion about the topic at hand. Clearly, there is no prohibition against discussing the restoration of women to the ordained diaconate, a tradition followed in the Eastern and Western churches for many centuries.

In 1987, Vagaggini was asked to make an intervention before the Synod of Bishops on the Laity, which had gathered 231 bishops and 60 lay auditors. The interventions ranged over a number of topics concerning the four major areas listed by the Synod's *relator*: (1) lay involvement in the secular world; (2) tensions between new lay ecclesial movements and their local churches; (3) lay ministries; (4) women in the church.[4] Among those speaking on this final area of interest were Milwaukee Archbishop Rembert Weakland, who asked that women be included in all non-sacerdotal ministries, and Vagaggini.

---

[2] Roger Gryson, *The Ministry of Women in the Early Church*, trans. Jean Laporte and Mary Louise Hall (Collegeville, MN: Liturgical Press, 1976); original: *Le ministère des femmes dans L'Église ancienne. Recherches et synthèses, Section d'histoire* 4 (Gembloux: J. Duculot, 1972); Aimé-George Martimort, *Deaconesses: An Historical Study*, trans K. D. Whitehead (San Francisco: Ignatius, 1986); original: *Les Diaconesses: Essai Historique* (Rome: Edizioni Liturgiche, 1982).

[3] Martimort, *Deaconesses*, 75.

[4] Seàn O'Riordan, "The Synod on the Laity," *The Furrow* 39, no. 1 (January 1988): 3–12.

Vagaggini's intervention, translated here, is strong both in response to Martimort and in explication of Vagaggini's own research. While Vagaggini's *Orientalia* article demonstrates the genuine nature of the ordinations of women to the diaconate in the Byzantine East and points to the possibility of women being included in the contemporary ordained diaconate, the long article is filled with technicalities and terms worthy of a formal Vatican document.

Vagaggini's Synod intervention as published in *Il Regno* can serve as an informal summary of his entire discussion. As it happened, there was no mention of women as deacons in the final Synod document, *Christifideles laici* (1988), which states that John Paul II's prior apostolic letter, *Mulieris dignitatem* (1988), ought to "enlighten and guide the Christian response to the most frequently asked questions, oftimes so crucial, on *the 'place' that women can have and ought to have in the Church and in society.*"[5]

A few years after the closing of the Synod on the Laity that resulted in *Christifideles laici*, the ITC formally took up the question of women as deacons. While a brief paper—fewer than twenty pages—was produced in 1997, it was not signed by its then-prefect, Cardinal Joseph Ratzinger, and not published. The ensuing *quinquinnaria* of the ITC, under a new working sub-group chaired by the single continuing member of the first sub-group (a former student of Ratzinger's), eventually produced a study document of nearly eighty pages, four times the size of the original document that apparently focused mainly on women in the diaconate.

The newer ITC document under consideration and eventually published expanded the discussion. The document strongly implies that the "iconic argument" (Christ was male) and gendered diaconates in history mitigate against returning women to the order of deacons. Even so, this later 2002 ITC study document notes that the question of including women in the restored

---

[5] John Paul II, Post-Synodal Apostolic Exhortation *Christifideles laici*, no. 50.

diaconate is something that the church's "ministry of discernment" should decide given that male and female deacons of history are not identical to deacons today and that the bishop and priest are clearly distinguished from the deacon.[6]

The ITC's 2002 study document, which remains the most recent direct Vatican discussion of women in the ordained diaconate, depends in part on Martimort. The study also depends heavily on prior published work by Gerhard L. Müller, who at the time was a member of the sub-committee preparing the ITC study.[7] Müller was nearly immediately named bishop of Regensburg following publication of the ITC study document, which position he held until being named prefect of the Congregation for the Doctrine of the Faith in 2012. He was reappointed by Francis.

At this time, the 2007 disciplinary document of the Congregation for the Doctrine of the Faith regarding sacred ordination of a woman remains in effect.[8] However, the discussion about the

---

[6] Benedict XVI's apostolic letter *Omnium et mentem* (2009) modified Canons 1008 and 1009, codifying what was already noted in the *Catechism of the Catholic Church*.

[7] Original in French: *Le Diaconat: Évolution et Perspectives*, published in English as *From the Diakonia of Christ to the Diakonia of the Apostles* (London: The Catholic Truth Society, 2003; Chicago: Hillenbrand Books, 2004) and recently added to the Vatican's website in German, Italian, Polish, Portuguese, and Spanish; http://www.vatican.va/roman_curia/congregations /cfaith/cti_documents/rc_con_cfaith_pro_05072004_diaconate_en.html (accessed November 12, 2013). Compare Gerhard Müller, *Priesthood and Diaconate: The Recipient of the Sacrament of Holy Orders from the Perspective of Creation Theology and Christology* (San Francisco: Ignatius Press, 2002), trans. Michael J. Miller from *Priestertum und Diakonat: Der Empfänger des Weihesakramentes in schöpfungstheologischer und christologischer Perspective* (Freiburg: Johannes Verlag, 2000).

[8] Congregation for the Doctrine of the Faith, *General Decree regarding the delict of attempted sacred ordination of a woman* (December 19, 2007); http:// www.vatican.va/roman_curia/congregations/cfaith/documents/rc_con _cfaith_doc_20071219_attentata-ord-donna_en.html (accessed November 13, 2013).

place of women in the church, and especially within ordained ministry, retains its vigor. Interestingly, the identical word for the "place" of women, *spazio*, has twice been used by popes since it appeared in *Christifideles laici*. In 2006, Benedict XVI asked if women could be offered more *spazio*;[9] in his August 2013 interview Francis said it was necessary to give women more space, more room, in the church.[10]

Below are translations of Vagaggini's Synod intervention as published in the Italian journal, *Il Regno*, and of Vagaggini's article from *Orientalia christiana periodica*. Each has been reviewed many times, but the inevitable errors are simply that and are not intended to misrepresent either Vagaggini or the discussion.

Phyllis Zagano

---

[9] Phyllis Zagano, "The Question of Governance and Ministry for Women," *Theological Studies* 68 (2007): 348–67.

[10] Antonio Spadaro, "A Big Heart Open to God," *America Magazine* 209, no. 8 (September 30, 2013): 15–38; see http://www.americamagazine.org /pope-interview (accessed October 15, 2013) for the sentences about women that do not appear in the printed journal.

"The Deaconess in the Byzantine Tradition"

By Cipriano Vagaggini

*Translated by Carmela Leonforte-Plimack
with Phyllis Zagano*

I have been asked to express my opinion about the possibility that the church, if it judges it appropriate, would be able to confer on women the sacrament of order in the diaconal grade. I have been requested[1] in particular to bear in mind the position A.G. Martimort has taken on this issue in his work *Les diaconesses; essai historique* (Rome: Ed. liturgiche, 1982). It is said that this work leads many to maintain that the church cannot admit women to the diaconal order. To try to clarify the above-mentioned issue, I will consider only the ordination of deaconesses in the Byzantine tradition, as I did in my 1974 article, "L'ordinazione delle diaconesse nella tradizione bizantina," *Orientalia christiana periodica* (vol. 40, 1974, pp.145–87). In that article I maintained, and I still maintain today, that the competent authority of the church, if it judges it appropriate, can admit women to the sacrament of order in the diaconate. The essential principles of my position are the following.

---

[1] A historical-liturgical contribution offered upon request to the synod fathers. —*Il Regno* editor

1) We know well the rite of the Byzantine tradition for the ordination of deaconesses. The oldest codex we have for this rite is the eighth-century Barberini Codex Gr. 336, known as the Barberini Euchologies. Then, with some slight variations in the rubrics, the same rite appears in a series of codices until the fourteenth century. As far as our issue is concerned, what has to be particularly noticed in this rite, apart from other details, is above all the fact that the ordination of deaconesses occurs and can occur only within the sanctuary (the *bemavima*, behind the iconostasis), at the foot of the altar. According to the Byzantine rite, ordination within the sanctuary only occurs (and today this is still the case) for the ordination of the bishop, the presbyter, the deacon, and the deaconess. Ordination to any other order, such as subdeacon, acolyte, etc., has always taken place, and even now takes place, outside the sanctuary—today, usually at the threshold of the entrance door to the sanctuary, but still outside of it.

2) Has this liturgical fact a precise significance? For a long time historians have not asked themselves this question. Instead, all things considered, the answer is given in the clearest manner by Theodore of Mopsuestia (born in Antioch c. 350 and died in Mopsuestia, Cilicia, in 428). He says, with regard to 1 Tim 3:8-15:

> It is worth adding that we should not be surprised if (Paul) mentions neither subdeacons nor lectors. In fact, these are outside of the grades in the ministry of the Church: created later because of the needs that had to be attended to by others (ministers) for the good of the great number of believers. Therefore, the law does not allow them to receive the *cheirotonia* (= imposition of the hands) in front of the altar because they do not minister the mystery; but lectors perform the readings and the subdeacons, inside [the sanctuary], take care of what is needed for the service by the deacons, as well as attending to the lights in the church. This is because only presbyters and deacons perform the ministry of the mystery—the former fulfilling their priestly office, the latter

administering the sacred things. (See *Theodori ep. mopsuest. in ep. B. Pauli comm.*, Cambridge 1880, vol. 2, pp. 132–34, and my article p. 182)

The text demonstrates that Theodore bears witness to the theological conviction that within the whole of "sacred orders" there exists a fundamental distinction between the group comprising bishop, presbyter, and deacon on the one hand and the group comprising lector and subdeacon on the other hand; and this distinction has its ritual expression in the ordinations, in the fact that the first group is ordained at the foot of the altar within the sanctuary-*vima* and the second not. The distinction, according to Theodore, has its origin in the fact that [those in] the first group (bishop, presbyter, deacon) are of apostolic origin and the others are not. Theodore does not speak about deaconesses in this context, but he knows them well and deems them of apostolic origin, as also did at that same time John Chrysostom and Theodoret of Cyrrhus (see my article, p. 183, footnote 2). The same is supposed in the Byzantine rite for the ordination of deaconesses, where the deaconess Phoebe, of whom St. Paul speaks in Rom 16:1-2, is mentioned.

According to this view we should say the following: first, in the perspective of the Byzantine church, as handed down in its rituals (*euchologi*) from the eighth century onwards, the ordination of deaconesses is considered, together with the presbyterate and the diaconate for men, what today we call a real sacrament (of diaconal order) and not a sacramental, much less a sort of blessing of a more or less ascetic type. It is pure fantasy to insinuate that it is only a sort of blessing for the purpose of an ascetic life. Second, by virtue of this sacrament, the order which deaconesses receive is what today we would call a major order, the last one of the group formed by the order of bishops, the order of presbyters, and that of deacons. To say that in the Byzantine rite of that time the feminine diaconate is something thoroughly different from the diaconate of men (Martimort, p. 155) is ambiguous and misleading. What is this thoroughly different thing?

In reality, of course, without saying that in the Byzantine tradition the diaconate of women was simply the same as the diaconate of men (here Martimort restates the obvious), we must say that in that tradition the diaconal order included two grades, one male and one female, with a very different range as far as their liturgical functions were concerned, but both of a strictly sacramental nature and as major orders.

3) At this point the question arises regarding the specific functions to which women who received the aforementioned feminine diaconal sacrament were entitled and ordained to. It is ambiguous and misleading to say that: "As long as the Byzantine tradition was kept alive it did not assign any liturgical duty to deaconesses" (Martimort, p. 250). Instead, in this area it is necessary to make two affirmations.

The first is that in Byzantium they were convinced that diaconal ordination *per se* allowed women to perform precise duties, even of a liturgical nature. In this sense the evidence of the civil-canonical legislation in the *Novella* of Justinian 6, 6 (535) is explicit. In this *Novella* the deaconesses' duties are described in sum as follows: "*To serve during sacred baptisms and be present in the other secret things that are customarily performed by them in the sacred mysteries.*" In this affirmation is included at least the liturgical task of anointing women's bodies during the conferring of baptism (which took place by immersion). This duty was well known throughout the previous Eastern tradition, as is shown, for example, by the *Didascalia* 3, 12 (third century), by the *Apostolic Constitutions* 3, 16, 2-4 and 8, 28, 6 (fourth century), by St. Epiphanius (*PG* 42, 744–45: *circa* 375), and by Severus of Antioch (*Letter* 62, *circa* 519–38).

The second affirmation is the observation that, notwithstanding the above-mentioned general and theoretical conviction, one notices on the practical level a tendency by which the liturgical functions of deaconesses in the Byzantine rite were effectively performed by men deacons or presbyters. In fact, this situation did not preclude the possibility for the deaconesses to perform the liturgical duties mentioned in the *Novella* of Justinian 6, 6, but rather rendered that possibility purely theoretical. And this carried with it the major disadvantage that the office of deaconesses, in itself truly a sacrament, tended to become purely theoretical and honorary.

4) At this point one might argue that in today's church the idea of reestablishing the ordination of deaconesses, following the path we have traced so far, is false because these deaconesses would in practice have no function, especially no liturgical function, in the life of the church today, as there is no longer baptism by immersion. The answer is that the situation has largely changed in the life of the present church, and as far as the extent of the tasks, even the liturgical tasks, of women the situation is also outdated. It is known, in fact, that today there are many cases, especially in Third-World countries, but not only there, where there are women who by indult in practice perform all the tasks, even of a liturgical nature, that a parish priest can perform, except to say Mass and to confess. And, let us not forget that Benedict XIV, when he approved *in forma specifica* (i.e., as a pontifical law) the Lebanese Maronite synod of 1736, allowed deaconesses of that rite (who at the time were usually abbesses of monasteries) among other things to give "extreme unction" to their nuns (see Mansi 38, col. 163–64). If that is the case, one senses the legitimacy and urgency for competent authorities to admit women to the sacrament of order of the diaconate and to grant them all the functions, even the liturgical functions, that, in the present historic moment of the church, are considered necessary for the greater benefit of believers, not excluding—as I personally maintain—if it is judged pastorally appropriate, equality between the liturgical functions of men deacons and women deacons.

d. Cipriano Vagaggini
19 October 1987

"The Ordination of Deaconesses in the Greek and Byzantine Tradition"

By Cipriano Vagaggini

Translated by Amanda Quantz with Carmela Leonforte[1]

PREMISES

1) Purpose

The current problem of "feminine ministries" is not about the theological possibility of a "ministry" generally given to women. Rather, it is the problem of their "ordained" ministry and of the nature of that ordination (sacrament or not?), of its duties, and of its relationship with other ordained ministries, especially the subdiaconate, diaconate, and presbyterate. We will only consider the problem of the possibility of an ordained women's diaconate.

This study seeks to make a historical contribution to the problem. It will not attempt to rewrite, not even in summary form,

---

[1] "L'ordinazione delle diaconesse nella tradizione greca e bizantina" by Cipriano Vagaggini was published in *Orientalia christiana periodica* 40 (1974): 146–89, under the editorial direction of Robert F. Taft, SJ, professor emeritus, Pontifical Oriental Institute, Rome. The translators gratefully acknowledge Father Taft's consultation on the present translation, as well as the assistance of Phyllis Zagano.

the general history of the institution of deaconesses and its relationships to those of widows and virgins.[2] In this history we
only want to bring to light any data that can be used in resolving
the aforementioned problem. Therefore, we will analyze the data
that are directly or indirectly liturgical, in my opinion more than
has been done thus far.[3] From the point of view that we are
proposing, there are two truly interesting ecclesiastical traditions: the Greek Byzantine and the Syriac (Nestorian, Monophysite, and Maronite). The Latin tradition seems to me to be much
less valuable for our purpose. Basically, in this field there is
neither an Egyptian nor an Armenian tradition.

2) The manner of presenting the question

Today we are impelled to ask the question in the following
manner: was the ordination (the χειροτονία) of deaconesses con-
ceived of as a sacrament or as a sacramental; as a major order
or a minor order? However, this approach to the question presupposes many things that are characteristic of later Western

---

[2] For this general history there are now two foundational works that take
into account earlier research and provide the bibliography. For the history
of the deaconesses, and of their relationship to the widows, virgins, and
abbesses, from their rise in the church to their disappearance: A. Kalsbach,
Die altkirchliche Einrichtung der Diakonissen bis zu ihrem Erlöschen (*Römische
Quartalschrift*. 22 Supplementheft). Freiburg I/B 1926. The author then
provided a later summary in the article *"Diakonisse"* in *Reallexikon für Antike
und Christentum* 4 (1959), 917–928. For the period through the sixth century,
and though it is with regard to the Greek and Latin tradition, the historical
problem was recently taken up again by R. Gryson, *Le ministère des femmes
dans l'Eglise ancienne*, Gembloux 1972. There is also a useful collection of
texts, although it is incomplete: J. Mayer, *Monumenta de viduis, diaconissis
virginibusque tractantia* (*Florilegium Patristicum*, fasc. 42) Bonn 1939.

[3] These deal more directly with the ordination of deaconesses: *Die
Geschichte der Diakonissenweihe*, in *Eine heilige Kirche* 21 (1939), 57–76; E. D.
Theodoros, " Ἡ «χειροτονία» ἤ «χειροτεσία» τῶν διακονισσῶν," *Theologia*
(Review of the Holy Synod of the Greek Church, Athens) 25 (1954) 430–469;
576–601; 26 (1955) 57–76.

theology: 1) The technical difference between a sacrament and a sacramental; 2) the distinction between major and minor orders and in which grouping each of the orders is placed; 3) the opinion that the minor orders (including the subdiaconate) are, or were, only sacramentals and not sacraments.[4]

All of this presents problems for which there are no simple solutions. Historically, it is known that the technical distinction between a sacrament and a sacramental, along with the assertion that the number of sacraments is seven, came about in the West only in the twelfth and thirteenth centuries. Without denying that earlier, both in the East and in the West, one can find some initial reflections that tend to distinguish between μυστήρια and μυστήρια, *sacramentum* and *sacramentum*, order and order: these are only a matter of initial signs that go in different directions and that lead to different lists.

From a theoretical point of view, today one usually says: the sacraments were instituted by Christ or by the Apostles and they function *ex opere operato*; the sacramentals were instituted by the church and they function *ex opere operantis* (*Ecclesiae*).[5] However, it is not shown how, for example, marriage as a sacrament was instituted by Christ or by the Apostles. Rather, the washing of the feet, according to John 13:1-15, was instituted by Christ, who instructed his Apostles to do likewise; but the church has considered this to be only a sacramental. Some among the so-called sacramentals (benedictions and constitutive consecrations), were considered to have effects *ex opere operato*.

---

[4] For a panorama of the history and the current status of the aforementioned questions, see, for example, *DTC, Sacramentaux* XIV I (1939) 465–482. See there also *Ordre* XI 2 (1932) 1298–1309, especially 1308–1309 and 1380–1381: the position of medievals and moderns on the problem of whether the minor orders are sacraments or only sacramentals.

[5] See, for example, *DTC, Sacramentaux*, pp. 470–475. To my knowledge, the expression *Opus operantis Ecclesiae* was consecrated for the first time in an official document in the encyclical of Pius XII *Mediator Dei* from 1947: *AAS* 39 (1947) p. 532.

As far as the sacrament of Order is concerned: it is well-known that the major scholastics commonly considered minor orders to be sacraments also. Subsequently, such was denied because it was said that the minor orders appear only later in church history and in a varied and changing manner in different regions. However, marriage as a sacrament also appears later. Commonly, both modern and ancient exegetes do not consider "the seven" in Acts 6 to have been what were later called the "deacons." From the viewpoint of the institution by the Apostles, the deaconesses are in no worse a state than the deacons or than the monarchial episcopate (Rom 16:1-2; Phoebe; I Tim 3:11 as interpreted by many ancient and modern authors; the testimony of Pliny the Younger in 111–113: see Kirch, *Enchiridion* n. 30).

Methodological conclusion: when seeking to discern the nature of the ordination of deaconesses in the ancient documents, one must guard against presupposing *a priori* the distinctions of medieval and modern theology between sacrament and sacramental, with major orders equaling sacraments, minor orders equaling sacramentals.

As the starting point for our research we will take the *Didascalia Apostolorum*, the original Greek text of which is said to have been written in Syria in the middle of the third century. My reason for doing so is that among the documents that we have today, it is in the *Didascalia* that deaconesses appear for the first time not only as a group clearly distinct from the "established" widows and virgins, but also as a ministry of the local church, whose pastoral and liturgical task is clearly determined as being parallel to the ministry of the deacons, albeit with more restricted roles. The text does not yet speak of the "ordination" of the deaconesses; however, had it not existed, the *Didascalia* established the premises for it. Moreover, the author insists in such a way as to persuade every bishop of the usefulness and necessity for each of them to have deaconesses in their churches [dioceses], leaving the sense that it is a question of an institution, I would say, not necessarily new to the church, but certainly not very widespread. (See III 12, 2.)

I

THE *DIDASCALIA* (mid-third century): THE DIACONATE OF WOMEN

LITURGICAL AND PASTORAL MINISTRY TO WOMEN.

1) The Foundational Texts[6]

a) II 26, 3-8: with the central passage 6. Context: Lay people must give a tenth, as well as the first fruits, to the bishops, presbyters and deacons, widows and orphans: just as in the Old Testament the Israelites gave them to the High Priest, the priests, and the Levites:

> II, 26, 3. These (the bishops) are your high priests; what the Levites once were now the deacons,[7] the presbyters, widows and orphans are. 4. For you the high priest is the Levite bishop: he is your teacher, and, after God, your father who regenerates through water; he is your prince and he is your chief, and your powerful king. And may he who reigns in place of God be honored like God, since the bishop presides over you as the image of God (*in typum Dei*). 5. On the contrary, the deacon is there as an image of Christ; therefore, may he be loved by you. 6. May the deaconess be honored by you as image of the Holy Spirit. 7. May also presbyters be considered by you as images of the Apostles. 8. Consider the widows and the orphans as images of the altar.

b) III 12-13. In my opinion, all of 13 must be considered as referring equally to deacons and deaconesses: something that is not noted often enough.[8] It emerges in 12, 1, as the general theme of 12 and 13, as well as in 13, 1, as the particular theme of all of

---

[6] Alistair Stewart-Sykes, ed., trans., *The Didascalia Apostolorum.* Turnhout, Belgium: Brepols, 2009.

[7] It seems that for the author the word "deacons" includes both deacons and deaconesses. See below II 26,6 as well as III 13, taking into account 13,1-2 and 12,1.

[8] Gryson, 1c., pp. 75–79 does not take into account *Did.* III 13,2–7 for deaconesses.

13. In each text the author speaks equally about deacons and deaconesses. Context: 12: it is extremely useful and practically necessary that every bishop have in his church not only deacons, but also deaconesses, for the ministry to women; 13: deacons and deaconesses, each within his or her area, must be at the service of the bishop with regard to the faithful and they must act with zeal and solicitude, with full agreement between them, as "two bodies in one soul."

> III 12: Therefore, bishop, make[9] permanent workers of justice (διακόνους) who may help your people for life. Elect and make deacons from among your people those whom you like[10]: the man so that he might take care of the many things that are necessary,[11] and the woman for ministry among women. There are things for which you may not send a deacon to women because of the pagans; however you will send deaconesses. 2. Also, for many other things a woman deaconess is required. First, when women step down into the water (for baptism); when they step down it is necessary that they be anointed with oil by the deaconess. When you cannot find a woman especially a deaconess, the man who is baptizing must anoint she who is being baptized. But where there is a woman present and especially a deaconess, decency requires that women are not seen by men. Except for the laying on of the hand you anoint only the head, as in the past priests and kings in Israel were anointed. 3. Likewise, when you impose your hand, anoint the head of they who are being

---

[9] The Greek has προχειρίζου. προχειρίζω means: to place before, present, choose, establish in an office, order. At least since the eighth century, it is a technical term for ordination. See Lampe's dictionary; the Greek index of the *Apostolic Constitutions*; J. Hanssens, *La form dans les ordinations du rit grec*, in *Gregorianum* 5 (1924) pp. 236–239.

[10] δοκιμάζεις = you have tried and chosen.

[11] In the *Didascalia*, the male deacon has a very significant place in the life of the local church and which overshadows that of the presbyters. Eye, agent, and right arm of the bishop, his duties are very extensive above all in the pastoral, charitable, administrative field. See, for example, II 28; 30; 31; 32:3; 34:3, 37:6; 42:1; 44 (important); III 8:1.4.

baptized, whether they be men or women. After that, when you baptize, or when you authorize deacons or presbyters to baptize, the deaconess as we have already said, anoints the women, but a man pronounces the invocation (ἐπίκλησις) of the Godhead. And when she who has been baptized emerges from the water, the deaconess receives her, teaches, and instructs her about how the seal of baptism must be kept intact in chastity and holiness. 4. Therefore we say that the ministry of the woman deaconess is highly desirable and utterly necessary because even the Lord Our Savior was served by women who served him and they were Mary Magdelene and Mary the daughter of James, and the mother of Joses and the mother of the sons of Zebedee. The deaconess will be necessary to you in other things, so they might enter the households of pagans where you cannot enter where there are believing women and to attend to those women who are ill and to bathe those who are recovering from illness.

III 13: Deacons should model their behavior on that of bishops and they should be more active than bishops. They should not love dishonest profit and they should be diligent in their ministry. Their number should be sufficient according to the number of faithful in the church so they may attend the elderly women who are ill, to brothers and sisters who are sick, so they may accomplish their ministry with dispatch. The woman will take care of women; the deacon, being a man, will take care of men and, when ordered by the bishops, he should be prepared and quick in moving for the ministry and the service. 2. Therefore may each one know about his or her own task and carefully fulfill it with concern. And you should be of one mind, as two bodies with one soul, so you will understand how large the diaconal ministry is. 3. As the Lord said in the Gospel: "whoever wishes to become great among you shall be your servant, and whoever wishes to be first among you shall be your slave; just as the Son of Man did not come to be served, but to serve, and to give His life as a ransom for many." Likewise, you deacons should do the same and when it is necessary in your ministry you will give your life for your brothers. Do not doubt this, because even our Lord did not hesitate when he served us as it was written in Isaiah: "To justify the righteous, performing well as service for many." 4. Therefore if the Lord of heaven and earth served us and bore everything for our sake, how much more must we do the same for our brothers; because we are all his followers and we have been given the same tasks as Christ. Also, in the gospels you will find how it is written that our Lord girt himself with a cloth and took water from the basin while we were all seated; he washed our feet and wiped them with a cloth. 5. In so doing he demonstrated brotherly love so that we also may do the same to each other. If therefore the Lord did that, you, deacons, do not hesitate to do likewise to the powerless and the sick because you are the workers of truth, encouraged by the example of Christ. May you then serve with love, not complaining or doubting, because in so doing you act according to the ways of men and not of God and at the end of your life you will be rewarded according to your ministry. 7. Therefore you deacons must visit all those who are in need. Let the bishop know about those who are distressed; you must be his soul and mind, ever strong and always obedient to him.

2) The Foundational Data

a) *The diaconal ministry in the church includes two branches: one masculine and the other feminine, for pastoral ministry to women.* The author's idea is to persuade the bishop that, for adequate diaconal service in his church, he needs not only men deacons but also women deacons. For the author, this diaconal ministry in the church includes two branches: one male and one female (III 12,1-2; 13,1). This is so that such a ministry be an adequate service as much for men as for women (III 13,1-2). As a result, the author treats the male and female diaconates in a parallel way. Nevertheless, the work of the deacon in the church, even if it generally exercised with regard to men, is much more extensive than that of the deaconess. The duties of the deaconess are restricted to ministry for women, and in cases in which natural decency or decency required by customs and environment would not easily allow the bishop, presbyter, or deacon to approach them.

b) *The liturgical work of the deaconess* is related to the baptism of women. According to the *Didascalia*, the person who is baptized, whether woman or man, is baptized completely naked and, even before baptism, is anointed with oil all over his or her body. The bishop anoints the person's head (III, 12,2). However, as for women, it is indecent that they be seen naked by a man, and therefore the deaconess performs the remaining anointings. But only "a man" and not the deaconess pronounces "the names of the invocation of the Godhead" over those same women who are then baptized. Women who thus baptized come out of the pool are then "received" by the deaconess, who is also responsible for instructing them about the obligations to preserve in chastity and holiness the seal of baptism received. It is well known that these two tasks, receiving the baptized and further instructing them, subsequently developed into the role of godfather and godmother.

c) *The pastoral work of the deaconess to assist women.* The *Didascalia* is far from focusing on the liturgical work of ecclesiastical ministries. Indeed, above all, it deals with their general pastoral work. For deaconesses, it is the visiting of and charitable help for Christian women who are sick or in need. The *Didascalia* signals above all the case of Christian women in domestic settings where there are still pagans (III 12,1.4113,1) and concerning whom, for that reason, the bishop was unable to send a deacon. From the advice of III 13, simultaneously given to the deacon and deaconess, one can glimpse the practical importance and great extent that this diaconal ministry of visiting and assisting the needy had in the ordinary life of the church. It is a task that should be fulfilled with the greatest solicitude and charity, under the direct responsibility of the bishop, whom the deacon or deaconess must notify about particular cases (III 13,1.7. *Cf.* II 30; 31): without doubt this is because he might make arrangements to distribute the alms of the Church (*Cf.* II 2,4; 25,2; 27,4; III 4,1-2). In this task, whoever carries out the diaconal ministry must function as the soul and mind of the bishop (III 13,7). The text reiterates for both the deacon and the deaconess what was said of the deacon alone in II 44.

d) *Limits of the work of the deaconess: no allusion to any Eucharistic work; prohibition against women teaching and baptizing.* There is no hint in the *Didascalia* to the way in which deaconesses were appointed and no hint of any of their tasks in the celebration of the Mass or concerning the Eucharist. In III 6,9, in the context of a discussion about widows, the author prohibits not only widows from teaching and baptizing, even if "constituted," but women in general.

A pagan wishing to be catechized by a widow, especially concerning the incarnation and passion of the Lord (III 5,3-6) must be referred to the rectors of the church. In order to teach such doctrines, one must do so with authority (*firmiter prout decet*). If a pagan heard them explained by a woman, the effect, the author seems to say, could run contrary to what the Christian woman would wish (III 5,6). "It is neither right nor necessary therefore that women should be teachers, and especially concerning the name of Christ and the redemption, fruit of His passion. You, women, and especially you widows, have not been appointed to teach" (III, 6,1-2). The reason for this affirmation: Christ did not send women to teach:

> . . . for Our Lord Jesus Christ, our teacher has sent forth us, the Twelve, to teach the people and all nations. With us there were some women disciples: Mary Magdalene, Mary the daughter of James, and the other Mary; but he did not send them forth with us to teach the people. Had it been necessary that women teach our Lord would have commanded them to teach together with us. (III 6,1-2)

According to the *Didascalia*, women must not baptize: "We do not approve of a woman baptizing, or that one should be baptized by a woman, for it is a transgression of the commandment, and a great peril to she who baptizes and to he who is baptized" (III 9,1). The author speaks cautiously: we do not approve; it is against the law; it is dangerous. He goes no further. Was the author thinking of what is defined in modern categories as certainly illicit and probably invalid? In any case, the negative position against women baptizing was certainly common in antiquity.[12]

What is the reason for this prohibition?: "If in fact women had been permitted to baptize, our Lord and Teacher Himself undoubtedly would have been baptized by Mary His mother, whereas He was baptized by John, like others of the people" (III 9,2).

Naturally, there remains the problem of the objective value of this argument, as well as of the argument referenced above about the prohibition against women teaching. But one finds an abundance of these arguments in the subsequent tradition. However, one understands how with similar premises, the author of the *Didascalia* certainly wanted deaconesses to anoint women at the moment of baptism, but he did not allow them actually to baptize them, reserving this task for a man.

e) *The rank of deaconesses: probably, among the "dignities," after the deacons and subjected to them, but before lectors and subdeacons.* Here one cannot go beyond likely conclusions. With regard to *agape*, *Didascalia* III 28 distinguishes within the church the laity from the *dignitates* (ἀξιώματα: II 28,5). Among the *dignitates*, there appear in the very same text: the bishop (priest, pastor), presbyters, deacons, and the lector. The *Didascalia* only mentions the subdeacon in II 34,3 in a context that does not discuss "dignity." But if one pays attention to the great importance that the author gives to deaconesses in the life of the church, and to the fact that he considers their ministry to women as parallel to the deacons' ministry to men, even if less extensive (III 12-13), one gets the impression that, for him, deaconesses occupy a place in the

---

[12] Tertullian, *De bapt.* 17 PL 1, 1328–29; *De praescrip.* 41 PL 2, 68. After the *Did.*, besides the *Apostolic Constitutions* which emphasize, too, the negative position as the *Did.*; the same negative attitude is found again in Epiphanius (*Haer.* 79.3 PG 42.744) and in Basil with regard to lay people in general (*Ep.* 188 can. 1 *PG* 32.668).

community that is clearly superior to that of lectors and subdeacons, who are mentioned only once, and in a wholly incidental manner.

Didascalia II 26,3-7 says that while one must honor the bishop as the image of God and the deacon as the image of Christ, the deaconess must be honored as the image of the Holy Spirit and the presbyters as the images of the Apostles. This text is partly explained by *Didascalia* II 28: the bishop is the image of God, the mouth of God (II 28,2-9); the deacons are images of Christ, because, just as one cannot draw near to God without Christ, likewise the laity must approach the bishop through the deacon:

> . . . the laity should have great confidence in the deacons so that they do not continually bother the prince (= bishop); rather through the ministers, that is to say the deacons, they should point out to him what they want; in fact, no one may go to the omnipotent God except through Christ; therefore everything the laity wants to do first should be made known to the bishop through the deacons and only after be done. (II 28,6)

The presbyters are the images of the Apostles because they are the council of the bishop and the curia of the church (II 28,4). The statement that the deaconess is the image of the Holy Spirit seems to contain the idea, later explained by the author of the *Apostolic Constitutions* II 26,5-6: because just as the Holy Spirit is the Spirit of Christ and does nothing without his desire, so, too, the deaconess must not do anything without the consent of the deacon; and just as it is not possible to believe in Christ without the Holy Spirit, so women must approach the deacon or the bishop through the deaconess.[13]

---

[13] These expressions have implications in the area of Trinitarian doctrine, which is not a topic to be explored here. However, before the Council of Nicaea, "subordinationist" expressions or images such as is found in *Didache* II.26 were not meant to signify anything other than that in the economy of salvation, in everything, Christ does the will of the Father and the Holy Spirit: "he will not speak on his own authority but whatever he hears he will tell you . . . because he will receive what is mine and he will announce

II

FROM THE DIDASCALIA TO THE APOSTOLIC CONSTITUTIONS
(end of the fourth century): THE FACT OF THE ORDINATION
OF DEACONESSES AND ITS IMPLICATIONS FOR THEIR
RELATIONSHIPS TO THE "CLERGY" AND THE "PRIESTHOOD."

Canon 19 of Nicaea, a text by Basil, and some texts by Epiphanius serve our purpose here.

1) Canon 19 of Nicaea and the ordination of deaconesses

This canon speaks explicitly of deaconesses, of their χειροθεσία, of their relationship to the laity in the Church. But the meaning of this text is highly debated.[14] In order to facilitate the commentary, we will number the sentences. We will provide the Greek text only of the last sentence, the meaning of which is controversial. Its precise translation will be the aim of the discussion.

> 1. Regarding the Paulinists who later took refuge in the Catholic Church, the view has been established that they must be rebaptized. 2. If any of them had previously been part of their clergy and if they appear to be blameless and irreproachable, after having been baptized they should be ordained (χειροτονείσθωσαν) by the bishop of the Catholic Church. 3. If, however, after an inquiry they are deemed unfit, they must be deposed. 4. Likewise, with regard to the deaconesses (ὡσαύτως δὲ καὶ περὶ τῶν διακονισσῶν) and generally with regard to those who are counted among the clergy, the same rule will be kept. 5. (Ἐμνήσθημεν δὲ τῶν διακονισσῶν τῶν ἐν τῷ σχήματι ἐξετασθεισῶν, ἐπεὶ μήτε χειροθεσίαν τινὰ ἔχουσιν, ὥστε ἐξάπαντος ἐν τοῖς λαϊκοῖς αὐτὰς ἐξετάζεσθαι.[15]

---

it to you" (John 16:13-14), and He is given to human beings only by Christ, to whomever Christ wishes and in whatever measure he wishes.

[14] A history of the interpretation is in Kalsbach Op. cit. pp. 46–49. For Gryson's interpretation see Gryson's Op. cit. pp. 86–87.

[15] The text presents just one textual question. In sentence 4, following Pope Gelasius, some Latin sources read: διακονῶν rather than διακονισσῶν (See Hefele-Leclercq, *Hist. des conc.* I/I p.616) against the other Greek

With regard to the fifth sentence, two recent scholars, Kalsbach and Gryson, believe that the Council makes a general affirmation that is valid for all deaconesses and in all cases: that is to say those deaconesses are not ordained and therefore always belong to the laity.

Other authors, ancient, from the seventeenth century, and modern, though with different shades of meaning, believe that the fifth sentence refers to one group of deaconesses and the fourth sentence to another group. They believe that the Council establishes that only those belonging to the group denoted in the fifth sentence do not receive ordination and therefore that they belong to the laity. But they maintain that, with regard to the deaconesses in the fourth sentence, the Council claims, firstly, that among the Paulinists they had already received ordination and they belonged to the clergy. Secondly, the Council allows that some of these deaconesses, having been rebaptized and having entered the Catholic Church—if they are found worthy— might eventually be ordained with the imposition of hands by the Catholic bishop and be numbered among the Catholic clergy, according to the general rule for Paulinist clergy, as explained in sentences two and three.

In my opinion, the first solution is untenable. The fundamental reason is that such an interpretation introduces a contradiction between sentences four and five. In fact, in any case, sentence four first affirms that the deaconesses of whom it speaks of are part of the clergy. In fact, it says "likewise about the deaconesses and, generally, about those who are included in the canon." Now, in the canons of Nicaea, to be included in the canon either means

---

sources. This reading appears too strongly as a correction in order to avoid the problem of the text and that of the supposed contradiction. In sentence five we maintain, along with the majority of editors, μηδέ instead of μήτε but it does not seem that the variation is significant because the terms also allow for an identical meaning.

or implies clerical status,[16] while in the above-mentioned inter-pretation, the text is made to say that each and every deaconess must simply be included among the laity.

Moreover, the same interpretation contradicts sentence four, insofar as this sentence affirms that, for the deaconesses of whom it speaks, the same rule must be observed as that established in the preceding context for the ex-Paulinists who had clerical status within that sect: these latter, in order to be admitted to the Catholic clergy first had to be rebaptized and then, if previously found worthy, receive ordination by a Catholic bishop. If, however, they were found unworthy, they were to be deposed. In my opinion, it is arbitrary to restrict the sense of "equally" (ὡσαύτως), as did Kalsbach and Gryson, in sentence four regarding deaconesses, as if it is meant to refer only to that part of the canonical rule of the Council according to which the ex-Paulinist clergy found unworthy were to be deposed, but excluding the other part, so that those found worthy could be ordained by the Catholic bishop and admitted to the Catholic clergy. Gryson[17] believes that the aforementioned restriction must be accepted because, he says, otherwise one cannot explain why, in sentence five, the canon says that deaconesses (Gryson means any deaconesses) do not receive ordination and therefore are always lay. However, the objection is precisely whether or not sentence five refers to all deaconesses.

Now, this sentence five, from a philological point of view, perfectly allows for a meaning that does not imply that it is a matter of each and every deaconess but only of a certain group among deaconesses: this removes every contradiction between sentences five and four. The boundaries of the fifth sentence allow it to be translated in the following way:

---

[16] Can. 17: many who "are within the canon" give themselves to usury. If, from now on, any of them does this again "that one is deposed from the clergy and removed from the canon." See also the beginning and end of Can. 16.

[17] Op. cit., p. 87.

Moreover,[18] we have dealt[19] with those deaconesses,[20] even if[21] not ordained, establishing that[22] they are to be counted among the laity.

Therefore, the text becomes understandable without any contradiction with regard to the preceding text and the whole canon appears to be logically constructed. The first sentence affirms the general rule that all Paulinists (Trinitarian heretics) who want to enter the Catholic Church must be rebaptized. Sentences two and three apply in particular to those ex-Paulinists who, within that sect, were part of the clergy. They presented the particular problem of whether, after they had been rebaptized, they could be admitted to the Catholic clergy. The synod states that an inquiry is to be made: if they are found worthy, the Catholic bishop may give them holy orders (and thereby admit them to the Catholic clergy). If, on the other hand, they are found unworthy, he must depose them from the clerical status that they had among the Paulinists. Sentence four determines that the preceding norm applies to deaconesses as well, and to other Paulinists

---

[18] δέ (ἐμνήσθημέν δέ) can have an adversative sense (rather, on the contrary), or continuous (at the same time, and then, more, besides).

[19] ἐμνήσθημεν: first person plural aorist middle as μιμνήσκω or of μνάομαι (which in different tenses have the same form): The meaning: 1. "to think" in general; 2. "to remember"; "to mention"; 3. "to deal with"; "to take care of." It can suggest a request or a command.

[20] τῶν διακονισσῶν τῶν ἐν τῷ σχήματι ἐξετασθεισῶν = of those deaconesses who are found within the schema, that is, in the habit, state, rank.

[21] ἐπεί: can mean: 1. A concept of time: when, after, while; 2. A sense of the cause of something: why, the motive for something; 3. A sense of consequences: therefore, so; 4. A concept of limitation: even though, nevertheless.

[22] ὥστε: consecutive conjunction (so that, in order to) with the infinite as the desired or possible outcome. It is often used with verbs that convey a desire, command, or decision. It occurs frequently in the structure of the canons of Nicaea (8;14;15;13;17): in the event that these or those situations occur, it determines or establishes that . . . ὥστε. In sentence five such volition or judgment can be implied in the verb ἐμνήσθημεν or in an implied verb, such as: we have dealt with deaconesses and decided that . . .

who were included in the canon, that is, those who were clergy. These "others" are at least the subdeacons and the lectors.[23] Among these deaconesses and other clergy, one can presume that they had received the Paulinist laying on of hands. In the canons of Nicaea the laying on of hands [*cheirothesia*] is the same as ordination [*cheirotonia*].[24]

Next, in sentence five, the synod analyzes another particular case: that of deaconesses who were such without having received the laying on of hands–ordination (*cheirothesia–cheirotonia*); the synod determines that such deaconesses, in any case, should simply be considered laity.

Therefore, the Council is aware that not all deaconesses received the laying on of hands. But does it presume this only among the Paulinists, or also among the Catholics? Certainly, at least among the Paulinists. From the text one cannot exclude that, according to the Council, the same thing occurred among the Catholics.

Against the interpretation we have explained Kalsbach makes one objection: backing such an interpretation, he says, causes the unverifiable hypothesis of the existence of two types of deaconesses: ordained and not ordained. One can respond, first and foremost, that it is not a matter of a hypothesis but of a fact implied by the same text and without which the text is incomprehensible because it is contradictory.

---

[23] From Can. 3 it is clear that for the Council of Nicaea, the clergy, besides the bishops, presbyters, and deacons, also included other male categories.

[24] One cannot verify that the ordination in sentence five is a different liturgical act than the ordination in sentence two and in canons 4, 8, 9, 15, 16. In the ancient documents *cheirotonia* (ordination) and *cheirothesia* (blessing) are not infrequently synonyms. Such is the case, for example, the Council of Chalcedon Can. 6: *Sacramentario di Serapione* n. 28 and n. 1 (ed. Funck, *Didiscalia . . .* II p. 190). See C. Vogel, *Chirotonie et chirothésie. Importance et relativité du geste de l'imposition des mains dans la collation des ordres*, in *Irénikon* 45 (1972) 7–21; 207–239. Other documents go on to expressly distinguish between *cheirotonia* and *cheirothesia*. See, for example, in *Apostolic Constitutions* VIII 28, 2–3. Therefore it must be that the distinction between *cheirotonia* and *cheirothesia*, if it exists, always results from individual documents.

If one then analyzes the historical context before and after Nicaea, one can notice the following. It is impossible to resolve the question of whether in the *Didascalia* the deaconesses were or were not considered part of the "clergy." But the author certainly considers them to be more important in the church than the lector who, nevertheless, for the author, belonged to the "dignities." We also know that the *Didascalia* is urging the bishops to resolve to institute a female diaconal ministry in their churches [dioceses]. This implies that such was not the usual practice. Moreover, the author does not speak of the liturgical ordination of deaconesses but rather presents their ministry as parallel, even if more restricted, to that of the deacons. All of this leads to the conclusion that it is not a rash hypothesis to think that, between the first half of the third century and the end of the fourth, that is, between the *Didascalia* and the *Apostolic Constitutions*—where deaconesses appear clearly as members of the clergy and are ordained with the laying on of hands—there was a period of transition: a period in which the practice of ordaining deaconesses and considering them clergy gradually spread, but was not necessarily imposed everywhere simultaneously. In this way, the position of the Council of Nicaea, as we have interpreted it, appears normal and logical as evidence, indeed, of such a state of things.

Moreover, as can be seen below with regard to Basil and Epiphanius, still around 374 and among the same Catholics, in Cappadocia deaconesses were not part of the clergy and therefore were not ordained with the laying on of hands. Rather, according to Epiphanius, they were certainly part of the ἐκκλησιατικὸν τάγμα below the subdeacons and lectors but before exorcists and, according to Gryson,[25] probably received ordination with the laying on of hands. Therefore, it is not an unwarranted hypothesis to suggest that the Nicene legislation in itself and as it was interpreted around 374 allowed for both possibilities.

[25] Op. cit. p. 134.

Finally, in the interpretation offered by Kalsbach and Gryson, it remains an enigma how, from the *Apostolic Constitutions* and subsequently, the usual Greek and Syriac custom, comprised of the great councils such as Chalcedon and Trullo, let alone civil legislation, could have accepted deaconesses who had been ordained and made part of the clergy without ever justifying the contradiction—if they ever did—of the Nicene canon.

The above at least demonstrates that the later tradition was not aware of contradicting a canonical rule of the Council of Nicaea, opposing the ordination of deaconesses and the fact of counting them among the clergy. The author of the *Apostolic Constitutions* in no way gives the impression of innovating anything in canonical practice.

2) Epiphanius of Salamis's understanding of the division of the ministries into two groups: "Hierosyne" and "after Hierosyne." The deaconess is not part of "Hierosyne."

Among the information that we have about deaconesses in the fourth century before the *Apostolic Constitutions*, let us note the following.

From Letter 199 of St. Basil to Amphilochius—the so-called canons of St. Basil[26]—from 375 one can see that for him the deaconess is bound to remain continent. If she is guilty of violating her "consecration" to a life of chastity, she is bound to do penance and is only to be readmitted to communion after seven years if, in the meanwhile, she has proven herself to be living a chaste life. This demonstrates that for Basil deaconesses are not part of the clergy. Indeed, in antiquity, for a grave fault, clergy were demoted to the laity, but never permitted to do public penance, according to the principal that someone must not be punished twice for the same fault (*Ap. Const.* VIII 47,25).

In the writings of Epiphanius of Salamis one finds a great deal of information about the existence, functions, obligations, and position of deaconesses in the church.

---

[26] Can. 44, *PG* 32, 370.

With regard to the proper ministry of deaconesses, Epiphanius says that this ministry pertains to women when required by decency: "Whenever a woman's body must be undressed, so as not to be seen by men in the sacred duties. . . ."[27]

Deaconesses must either be married to only one man, observing continence, or they must be widows who were only married once, or perpetual virgins. These are the same obligations imposed on bishops, presbyters, deacons, and subdeacons.[28]

According to Epiphanius, deaconesses were certainly "constituted" (καθίσθημι).[29] But how? It is likely, but not certain, that Epiphanius was familiar with the ordination of deaconesses by the laying on of hands.[30]

The newest thing Epiphanius says is about the relationship between deaconesses and ἱερωσύνη. In *Contra Haereses* (374–377), Epiphanius says that the highest level (τάξεις) in the church is comprised of the ἱερωσύνη: "it is like the mother and parent of

---

[27] *Haer.* 79, 3 PG 42, 744–745. See also *Ibid. Exposit. fid.* 21 PG 42, 824–825.

[28] See *Expos. fid.* 21 PG 42, 824–825.

[29] Ibid. 824 C.

[30] In a letter preserved in Jerome's Latin translation, Epiphanius defends himself against John of Jerusalem—considered by him to be adhering to the "Origenist heresy"—of having ordained (*ordinavimus, ordinavi*) someone a deacon and then presbyter and then having sent him to Palestine to a monastery: *fratrum, et fratrum peregrinorum, qui provinciae tua nihil debuere* (*CSEL* 54, 396, 4–5). Then, he adds, it seems in order to defend himself from the accusation of having "ordained" deaconesses and likewise sending them to Palestine: *numquam autem ego ordinavi diaconissas et ad alienas misi provincias neque feci quidquam ut ecclesiam scinderem* (*Ibid.* 398, 11–13). The fact that in that letter the Latin uses the same word *ordinavi* for presbyters, deacons and deaconesses could indicate that the original Greek also used a single term. But one cannot be entirely sure, even if it is likely, that the term was χειροτονέω or not, for example, the simple κατίσθημι. In the fragments of the Latin translation of Hippolytus completed more or less in the same period as Epiphanius (last quarter of the fourth century, according to Botte): *ordinare* translates as χειροτονεῖν in n.2 p.4; n.7 p.20. At the beginning of n.8 p.22 where the Latin has *ordinatur* (the deacon) Sahidic Coptic has κατίσθαι; but the Sahidic text does not seem to be accurate. Finally, the same n.8, *ordinatur* resonates with χειροτονεῖν.

the other levels."[31] To the ἱερωσύνη belong: bishops, presbyters, deacons and subdeacons. "After the ἱερωσύνη" are: lectors, deaconesses, exorcists, interpreters, buriers, doorkeepers, and all those upon whom it is incumbent to maintain good order in the church.

One will note that this is an attempt to distinguish church ministers according to two neatly divided groups: something more or less analogous to what elsewhere and later was called major and minor orders.

For Epiphanius, therefore, deaconesses are not part of the ἱερωσύνη; it is not for them to exercise clerical functions (ἱερατεύειν).[32] Nevertheless, they belong to the ἐκκλησιαστικὸν τάγμα.[33] The expression seems to be a general term that covers both ἱερωσύνη or ἱερατικὸν τάγμα,[34] as well as what Epiphanius lists in the *Expositio fidei* after ἱερωσύνη. Nevertheless it is not clear whether in Epiphanius' use of the term ἐκκλησιαστικὸν τάγμα is the same as κλῆρος or κληρικοί.[35]

Among the Fathers Epiphanius is the one who predominantly developed the argument against the ἱερωσύνη of women in contrast to the practice of some Montanist sects and of the Collyridian sect.[36] He states that among the Montanists: "There are women

---

[31] *Haer., Exposit. fid.* 21 PG 42, 821–825.

[32] *Haer.* 79, 3 PG 42, 744.

[33] Ibid. 79, 4 PG 42, 745.

[34] Ibid. 75, 7 PG 42, 513 C.

[35] Rather, it is clear in Can. 6 of Chalcedon (451). In Epiphanius and contemporary and earlier authors (see κληρικοί in Lampe's dictionary) the terminology is not univocal, nor are the conclusions about κλῆρος and κληρικοί and the foundations on which they are based. The "clergy" sometimes includes: bishops, presbyters, deacons (*Haer.* 68,3 PG 42, 189 A); sometimes presbyters, deacons, "and others" (Ibid. n. 2 PG 42, 185 A); sometimes they simply seem to be opposed to "laity" or the "crowd" (τάγμα: Ibid. col. 186 D–188 A); sometimes it also seems to include ascetics and "virgins" (Ibid. n.4, col. 189 C.).

[36] *Haer.* 49 and 79 PG 41, 880–881; 42, 740–756.

bishops, presbyters, *et cetera* because, they say, indeed in Christ there is no difference; neither male nor female."[37]

Epiphanius' arguments against these abuses amount to the following: 1. The fact that in the Hebrew Bible, the New Testament, and the Christian tradition there is no female priesthood. 2. The main issue is the fact that Christ did not make Mary a priest, nor did he give her the task of baptizing, which he certainly would have done and should have done if he had wanted women priests in the church. 3. Women are fragile, weak, and rather unintelligent. 4. He turns to some biblical passages: Gen. 3:16; I. Cor. 11:8; 14:34; I Tim. 2:14.

Epiphanius' statements about the role of the deaconess with regard to the ἱερωσύνη raise the problem, among others, of what exactly the concept of ἱερωσύνη is for the bishop of Salamis. Here one wonders in particular about the basis for his assertion that the subdeacon belongs to the ἱερωσύνη and that the lector does not belong to it.[38] It is certainly not because of less "sacred" duties. The subdeacon in the Eastern tradition is rather the equivalent of the acolyte in the Western tradition. One might consider their commitments to continence.

Why isn't the deaconess in the ἱεροσύνη at least equal to, though above, the subdeacon? According to Epiphanius himself, her duties pertaining to the baptism of women are, shall we say, more sacred, because they are more sacramental than those of the subdeacon or lector. Also, with regard to continence, the commitments of the deaconess are equal, if not greater than,

---

[37] *Haer.* 49, 2 PG 41,881 A.

[38] One can note this in connection to the case of the canons of the Council of Laodicea (343–381). These do not speak of deaconesses. However, the ecclesiastical groups are divided in this way: 1. The ἱερατικοί (ἱερατικὸν τάγμα): presbyters and deacons (the bishop seems to be outside of the list); 2. The others τῆς ἐκκλησιαστικῆς τάξεως = ὑπηρέται, lectors, singers, exorcists, ushers; 3. The τάγμα τῶν ἀσκητῶν; 4. The laity. See canons 24, 27, 36, 41, 42, 54.

those of the bishop, presbyter, deacon, and subdeacon. These questions are not resolved by Epiphanius.[39]

III

THE *APOSTOLIC CONSTITUTIONS* (end of the fourth century): THE DEACONESS AS AID TO THE DEACON WITH REGARD TO WOMEN, BUT, AS FOR THE IMPORTANCE OF MINISTRY SHE IS CLOSER TO THE DEACON THAN TO THE SUBDEACON OR LECTOR EVEN HAVING THE SAME ORDINATION.

Apart from the virgins and widows, the *Apostolic Constitutions* often speak about deaconesses.[40] Then, comparing texts that, in this field, the *AC* have in common with the *Didascalia* and those which they have independently, one can see the difference between the two. The *AC* fundamentally follow the route of the *Didascalia*, but in it the female diaconate appears as a self-evident, common institution in the region for which the *AC* were written, with some details that are more precise compared with the *Didascalia*, especially with a clear rite of ordination (*cheirotonia*) that is accompanied by a precise text.

1) Liturgical functions of the deaconess: baptism of women and the welcome and oversight of women in the liturgical assembly

In the *Didascalia* the function of deaconesses is above all to help the bishop or the presbyter in the baptism of women, because of decency.[41] While it rests with the bishop to anoint the head of every person being baptized, man or woman, by laying

---

[39] Other information about deaconesses around the end of the fourth century and before the *Apostolic Constitutions* provides some details that are of general interest for the history of the institution. However, they do not offer any new information about our theme. See Gryson Op. cit. pp. 135–142; 146–150.

[40] II 26,3–6; 57,10; 58,6; III 8,1; 11,3; 16; 19; VI 17,4; VIII 19–20; 21,2; 28,6–8.

[41] III 16,2.4; VIII 28.6.

his hand on the person's head, and it rests with the deacon to anoint the forehead, and it is the task of the deaconess to anoint the woman's whole body. But only the bishop or the presbyter says the words of invocation (ἐπίκλησις) in which, in order to baptize, he names the Father, Son, and Holy Spirit.[42]

After baptism, the deacon "receives" the men, the deaconess the women.[43]

Compared with the *Didascalia* the *AC* entrust deaconesses with an additional active task in the liturgical gathering: that of welcoming the women who enter the church, monitoring the respective doors, especially taking care of strangers and the poor and assigning everyone a place if necessary; the deaconess must behave like a ναυστολόγος, that is, as we might say today, like a *steward* or *stewardess* of a ship: work that they share with the porters or even with the subdeacons and deacons.[44]

2) Insistence on and new arguments about the limits of the work of deaconesses

One of the constant concerns of the *AC* is to define carefully the respective duties of individual ministries.[45] The *AC* reiterate and emphasize what the *Didascalia* said about the prohibition of women in general "to teach in the Church[46]: By no means did the Lord send women to preach (εἰς τὸ χήρυγμα)." It also adds a new argument: "if the man is head of the woman (I *Cor* 11, 13) it is not right that the rest of the body should govern the head."[47]

---

[42] III 16, 2–4.

[43] III 16, 4. The *AC* drop what the *Didascalia* added at this point: it is the task of the deaconess to "receive" the baptized women, and educate and teach them that the seal of baptism cannot be broken, but it must be kept intact in chastity and in holiness (*Did.* III 12,3).

[44] See II 57, 10; 58, 6; VIII 20,1; VIII 11,11.

[45] See III 10–11; VIII 28:46.

[46] III 6.

[47] III 6, 2.

This same argument, as well as others, helps the author of the *AC* to reinforce everything that the *Didascalia* had said about the general prohibition against women baptizing. If it was dangerous and illegal according to the *Didascalia*, for the *AC* it becomes nothing less than "impious."[48] Why? Here are the reasons:

> 2. If, in fact, "the man is the head of the woman" and the man is elected for the priesthood (προχειρίζεται εἰς ἱερωσύνην), it is not right to disregard the order of creation (δημιουργίαν), and abandon the source (ἀρχή) from which it is derived in favor of the body. In fact, the woman is the body of the man, is taken out of his side and is subjected to him from whom she is derived for the procreation of children. For it is said, in fact, "He shall rule over you." The man is the source (ἀρχή) of the woman and is therefore her head. 3. If as above, therefore, we do not allow women to teach how would it be possible to allow them against nature (παρὰ φύσιν), to fulfill priestly actions (ἱερατεύσαι)? This is the mistake of the impiety of pagans and not Christ's law: to ordain women priests (ἱερείας χειροτονεῖν) to the goddesses. 4. Had it been necessary to be baptized by women our Lord certainly would have been baptized by his Mother and not by John; or, as he sent us (the Apostles) to baptize, he would have sent together with us women for the same purpose. On the contrary, he never ordered this in any way and he did not hand it down in writing since he knew both the necessities of nature (τὴν ἀκολουθίαν τῆς φύσεως), and the requirements of decency because he is the creator of nature and the legislator of the natural order.[49]

In comparison with to what one reads in the *Didascalia*, what is noteworthy above in the *AC* is the insistence on a new argument: that because of φύσις and δημιουργία, by nature, women are inferior to man and the head of the woman is man, since she was formed from man and made so that he might have children. Now, the author supposes, to teach and to baptize means to

[48] III 9.1.
[49] III 9.1–4.

exercise superiority. Therefore, these acts are contrary to the nature of woman.

It is also worth noting the reference to the connection between female priesthood and female divinity among the pagans.[50]

However, for the author of the *AC*, baptizing is an act reserved for the bishop or, with the permission of the bishop, for the presbyter. Not only is it impermissible for lay people to do it,[51] it is not even permissible "for other clergy . . . such as lectors, cantors, porters, attendants (ὑπηρέται), only for bishops and presbyters with the help of deacons."[52]

As a matter of fact the *AC* have an entire paragraph that seeks to delimit neatly the respective liturgical duties of the bishop, presbyters, deacons, deaconesses, and subdeacons.

> VIII 28,2: A bishop blesses (εὐλογεῖ) he is not blessed; he imposes hands (χειροτονεῖ), offers [the sacrifice], (προσφέρει), receives the blessing (εὐλογίαι)[53] from the bishops but not from the presbyters; the bishop removes every cleric who deserves to be removed, except for a bishop, whom he cannot remove by himself. 3. The presbyter blesses (εὐλογεῖ), is not blessed, he receives the blessing εὐλογίαι from the bishop or from another presbyter, he extends his hand for the blessing, but he does not impose his hand for the ordination (χειροθετεῖ, οὐ χειροτονεῖ); he does not remove his inferiors, but he excommunicates them if they are liable to such a punishment. 4. The deacon does not bless (εὐλογεῖ); does not distribute the Eucharist εὐλογία, but he receives it from the bishop or from the presbyter;[54] he does not baptize, he does not offer the sacrifice (προσφερεῖ); but when the bishop or the presbyter have offered the sacrifice he distributes the Eucharist to the people but

[50] The same fear seems to be underlying in everything Epiphanius says about the Collyridians, *Haer*. 79 PG 42, 740–756.

[51] III 10.

[52] III 11.1.

[53] The εὐλογία is what remains of the offerings presented by the faithful for the Mass, which is not consecrated. See VIII 31.2.

[54] However, according to VIII 31.2 the deacon distributes the εὐλογίαι by order of the bishop or the presbyter.

not as the priest does (ἱερεύς), rather, because he is the servant (διακονούμενος) of the priests.[55] 5. It is not permitted to anyone among the other clerics to perform what pertains to the deacon. 6. The deaconess does not bless (εὐλογεῖ) and she does not do anything that is done by presbyters and deacons, but it pertains to her to guard the doors and to minister to presbyters in the baptism of women for the sake of decency. 7. The deacon excommunicates the subdeacon, the lector, the cantor, the deaconess if necessary in the absence of the presbyter. 8. The subdeacon is not permitted to excommunicate the lector, nor the cantor, nor the deaconess, nor the cleric, nor a lay person. In fact, they are ministers (ὑπηρέται) to the deacons.

In VIII 46 one notes again clearly how the author of the *AC* was very concerned about the matter of the precise delimitation of hierarchical tasks, especially in the liturgical field. One can see that this insistence has a polemical emphasis, specifically against the tendency of some deacons to overstep the boundaries of their ministry in order to assume presbyteral functions. Canon 18 of Nicaea had already strongly challenged this tendency.

3) The extra-liturgical duties of the deaconesses: to assist women and to be their mediators to the bishop and the deacon.

How, with regard to the work of the deaconess, the *Didascalia* places the primary emphasis on offering assistance to believing women, especially those who are ill and in need.[56] *AC* III.19, which describes the zeal and spirit that must animate the "deacons" in the aforementioned ministry, is addressed equally to deacons and deaconesses in a way that is more explicit and insistent than in the *Didascalia*.

---

[55] The other duties of the deacon in the Mass are described in VIII 6–15; at vespers and morning prayer in VIII 35.2–39.

[56] III 16, 1; 19, 1–7.

> Let the woman (deaconess) be zealous in taking care of women
> and let both (deacon and deaconess) be zealous in carrying mes-
> sages, in traveling away from home, in assisting, in serving, as
> Isaiah said of the Lord: the righteous one will be justified because
> he has well served the many (Isa 53:11). Let everyone then rec-
> ognize his or her proper task, let each accomplish it with zeal,
> with one mind, with one soul, knowing what is the reward of
> their service [as deacons and deaconesses].[57]

And so, the rest of the discourse is addressed both to deacons
and deaconesses, no less than the recommendation to do everything under the direction of the bishop: "you deacons must visit
all those who are in need of a visit and you must report to your
bishop about those who are afflicted, since you must be his soul
and his mind."[58] All of this considerably emphasizes the paral-
lelism of the deacon for men and the deaconess for women in
charitable extra-liturgical ministry as messengers and instru-
ments of the bishop.

Moreover, in the *AC* there appears another extra-liturgical
ministry of deaconesses: serving as mediators and accompany-
ing women when they need to speak with the deacon or the
bishop: "And as we cannot believe in Christ without the teaching
of the Holy Spirit, so let no woman address herself to the deacon
or bishop without the deaconess."[59]

4) Deaconesses are clearly part of the clergy

This is certain for the *AC* VIII 31,2: "the deacons, at the behest
of the bishop or of the presbyters, distribute to the clergy the
offerings that remain from the mystical oblations: to the bishop,
four parts; to the presbyter, three parts; to the deacon, two parts;

---

[57] III 19,1–2.

[58] III 19,7.

[59] II. 26.6. The bishop is the image of the Father, the deacon of Christ, the
deaconess of the Holy Spirit.

and to the rest of the sub-deacons, or readers, or singers, or deaconesses: one part."

Deaconesses are ordained by ordination (*cheirotonia*) just as is the bishop, the presbyter, the deacon, the subdeacon, and the lector. Neither virgins, nor widows, nor exorcists receive ordination (*cheirotonia*).[60]

On the rank of the deaconess among the other clergy one observes the following: according to the *AC* VIII 28,2-8, especially 7 and 8, the deaconess is clearly included, along with the subdeacons, lectors, and cantors, among the attendants (ὑπηρέται) of the deacon. The deaconess as attendant of the deacon in ministry to women also emerges from II 26,6. Here the statement of the *Didascalia* that the deaconess is the image of the Holy Spirit is explained in this way: while the bishop is the image of the Father, the deacon is the image of Christ: because as Christ served the Father and did nothing without him, so, too, the deacon serves the bishop and may do nothing without him. The deaconess is the image of the Holy Spirit: "because she neither says nor does anything without the deacon, just as the paraclete neither says nor does anything alone, except to glorify Christ, he abides by his will."

One cannot obtain a firm answer for the further question of whether deaconesses, who have the rank of clergy according to the *AC*, come right after deacons, subdeacons, or even after the other clergy.[61]

---

[60] In the extant text of the *AC* the subdeacon is noted only once in book eight, which, on the other hand, is not familiar with the porters who appear in books two, three, and six. While the *Didascalia* is familiar with the subdeacon, books two, three, and six of the *AC* mention the ὑπηρέται, unknown to book eight (since VIII 28,8 does not seem pertinent). In conclusion: in terms of the name, function and rank of subdeacons, porters, and the ὑπηρέται, there does not seem to be unity in the *AC*.

[61] A series of texts place the deaconesses right after the deacons and before the subdeacons; above all in the order in which the various ordinations are presented: bishops, presbyters, deacons, deaconesses (VIII 19), subdeacons, and lectors. VIII 2–8 has: bishop, presbyter, deacon, deaconess, subdeacon;

5) What is the nature of the ordination of deaconesses in the *AC*?

a) *The ordination of deaconesses*. The *AC* VIII 28,1-3 distinguish very neatly χειροτονία, χειροθεσία, εὐλογία. Only the bishop can do all three of these. The presbyter can do the second and the third, but not the first. The deacon (and even more so for those after him) cannot do even the third. Ordination is the same as ἐπίθεσις τῶν χειρῶν (*AC* III 10,2; VIII 46,9), that is to say: a laying on of hands with physical contact. Blessing (*cheirothesia*) is an extension of the hand without physical contact with the one being blessed (*AC* VIII 37, 4.39, I). The εὐλογία seems to be a simple prayer or formula for benediction that can also be done without the extension of hands over the one involved, since the author of the *AC* insists that the deacon is permitted to do "neither ordination, nor εὐλογία, neither minor nor major" (VIII 46,11. Cf. III 10,1).

The deaconess is made through ordination (*chierotonia*) that is to say (G) strictly reserved only for the bishop (VII 19,2; III 11,3).

During this rite the "presbyter, the deacons and the deaconesses" must be present (VIII 19.2).

The following is the blessing that the bishop says over the deaconess:

> O, Eternal God, Father of our Lord Jesus Christ, creator of man and of woman, you who have filled with your Spirit Miriam and Deborah, Anna and Hulda; you who have not deemed it unworthy that your only begotten Son be born of a woman; you who instituted women as guardians of the holy parts of the tent of the covenant and of the temple; You, even now, look upon this [female] servant of yours elected to the diaconate; grant her the

---

in III 11:3 it says "we do not allow the presbyter to ordain with the laying on of hands (χειροτονεῖν) neither deacons nor deaconesses, lectors, ὑπηρέται, cantors, nor doorkeepers." But in other texts deaconesses are named after all of the male members of the clergy: II 26:3, VI 17:1–4; VIII 28:7–8. See especially VIII 31, 2–3.

Holy Spirit and purify her from all sins of the flesh and of the spirit: so that she might fulfill the task entrusted to her for your glory and for the glory of your Christ, with whom and with the Holy Spirit, glory and adoration be to you and forever and ever.

Therefore, the above is substantially a prayer that the deaconess might receive the gift of the Holy Spirit in order to fulfill worthily the ministry of the diaconate that was entrusted to her. However, other than doorkeeping, what this ministry consists of does not emerge. But, as usually occurs in the liturgy—as with Hippolytus' *Apostolic Tradition*—the ministry of deaconesses is seen against the background of salvation history: inasmuch as one reads in the Old Testament and New Testament about instances in which the movement of God, now done in the church, in its own way appears to be ongoing. In the Old Testament, the aforementioned prayer refers to the prophetesses and to the female doorkeepers in the tent of the Covenant and the temple (Exod 38:8; I Sam 2:22). For the New Testament, recall that the Son of God did not find disdain in being born of a woman.

One could wonder why the prayer makes no mention of the case of Phoebe (Rom 16:1-2), nor of I Tim 3:11, nor numerous other and important liturgical and extra-liturgical tasks that the *AC* also identify with the deaconess. On the whole, the theology of this prayer is poorer than the theology that results from the picture of the deaconess illustrated in the *AC*. This possibly confirms that the aforementioned prayer is not an innovation on the part of the author of the same *Constitutions*.

b) *Comparison between the ordination of deaconesses and other ministers.* We have already observed above that the author of the *AC* distinguishes clearly between the ordination of deaconesses and the "constitution" of virgins and widows. These latter do not receive ordination; they do not belong to the clergy. Virginity and widowhood, for the *AC*, are not ministries, but ascetic and spiritual states of life (VIII 24.25). Not even the exorcist receives ordination; it is a charism in the modern sense, not a ministry (VIII 26).

There is no agreement among the extant text of the *Apostolic Constitutions* in the number of the ministers who are subordinate to the subdeacon, nor of the reality of whether these do or do not receive ordination.

In books II–VII the ministers are: the bishop, presbyter, deacon, deaconess, attendant (ὑπηρέτης), the cantor (ψάλτης, ᾠδός, ψαλτῳδός), the usher (πυλωρός) ([62]). According to III 11,3, all of these receive the ordination that is reserved only for the bishop: "we do not allow presbyters, but only bishops to give ordination (χειροτονεῖν) to the deacons, or the deaconesses, or the lectors, or other attendants, or cantors or ushers; this is the rule (τάξις) and ecclesiastical harmony."

On the other hand, in book VIII, the list is: bishop, presbyter, deacon, deaconess, subdeacon (ὑποδιάκονος, which seems to be the same as the ὑπηρέτης of earlier books), and lector. They all receive ordination (VIII 16-22). The ushers no longer appear in book VIII. The deacons, deaconesses and subdeacons now guard the doors (VIII 11,11; 20,1). Rather, the same book frequently speaks about cantors (10,10; 12,43; 13,14; 28,7-8; 31,2; 47,26.43.69). And it is certainly the case that also in Book VIII, the cantors are clergy distinct from lectors (VIII 31,2; 47,26). But here it does not speak of ordination, let alone the ordination (*cheirotonia*) of cantors.

The above is further evidence of the nature of compilation of the extant text of the *AC*, which is not always consistent.

Between the ordination of the deaconess and that of the bishop, presbyter, deacon, subdeacon, and lector in book VIII of the *AC*, one cannot find any difference with regard to the minister (bishop), the act of the laying on of hands, and the general structure of the prayer that accompanies it. In that respect, it would not make sense, with regard to book VIII, to distinguish between

---

[62] The order of these is not always the same. III 11.1 has: lector, ψάλτης, usher ὑπηρέτης. In III 11.3: deacon, deaconess, lector, ὑπηρέτης, cantor, usher.

major orders and minor orders among the aforementioned ministers, or even between sacraments and sacramentals.

However, it is important to guard against, with the typical Western mentality, the *a priori* belief that if one cannot find any distinction among the various ordinations in regard to the aforementioned points, the question is thus resolved in the sense that, in reality, such a distinction was not made. One cannot rule out, *a priori*, that such a distinction came to be perceived and expressed in other circumstances of the same rite.[63]

In fact, in the text of the *AC* itself, one must attend to the following points: The bishop is ordained by two or three other bishops in the presence of the presbyterate and the ministry of the deacons (VIII 4,6; 47,1). The presbyter is ordained only by the bishop in the presence of the presbyters and deacons (VIII 16,2). The deacon is ordained by the bishop alone in the presence of the presbyterate and the deacons (VIII 17,2). The deaconess is ordained only by the bishop in the presence of the presbyterate, deacons, and deaconesses (VIII 19,2). The subdeacon and the lector are ordained by the bishop alone, but nothing is said about the presence or absence of the presbyterate, deacons, deaconesses, subdeacons, or lectors (VIII 21.22). This detail should capture our attention. We know, in fact, from the earliest euchologies (eighth through eleventh centuries) that the ordination of subdeacons and lectors, in contrast to that of bishops, presbyters, deacons, and deaconesses, was done in the *diakonikón*, that is to say the sacristy, and not in public in front of the altar in the sanctuary. The fact that it was not done in the sanctuary in front of the altar, as occurred, rather, for the bishops, presbyters, and deacons, is testified to be a law by Theodore of Mopsuestia, a contemporary of the *AC*.[64] Therefore, there is legitimate

---

[63] From a text by Theodore of Mopsuestia (350–428), we know that it was prohibited to ordain subdeacons and lectors in front of the altar, as instead one was supposed to do for the bishop, presbyter and deacon. See below and pages 51–52.

[64] See below and pages 51–52.

suspicion that there is a trace of this same law in the *AC* when in the ordination of subdeacons and lectors the text is silent about the presence of the presbyterate, deacons, subdeacons, and lectors. Equally, there is legitimate suspicion that when the *AC* direct the ordination of the deaconess to occur in front of the presbyterate, deacons, and deaconesses (VIII 19,2), that the text presupposes that such ordinations be done in public and at the foot of the altar within the sanctuary, as those of bishops, presbyters, and deacons. However, even with regard to the presence of the presbyterate, deacons, and deaconesses, the ordination of deaconesses in the *AC* appears to be assimilated more with that of the presbyters and deacons than with that of the subdeacons and lectors.

Furthermore, one must pay attention to the extent and importance of the ministerial work that was assigned in each respective ordination. Now, according to the *AC*, the work of the deaconess is certainly inferior to that of the deacon, even if parallel to the same, because she is the aid of the deacon in ministry to women. But her work is much higher than that of the subdeacon and lectors, even if the deaconess, as a woman, did not read Scripture in the public assemblies. From this point of view, the ordination of deaconesses in the *AC* appears even closer to that of the deacon than to that of the subdeacon.[65]

Regarding the obligations of celibacy and continence, the *AC* require more from the deaconess than from the other clergy, presbyters and lower. According to the *AC* VI 17,1-4 the deaconess must be a "pure virgin or otherwise a monogamous widow, faithful and honorable" (VI 17,4), while after ordination the attendants (ὑπηρέται), cantors, lectors, and doorkeepers may still

---

[65] From a theoretical point of view it will be noted that the fact of being a helper to the deacon and of having less extensive duties than he is not an argument against the nature of sacrament of the female diaconate. The presbyter, too, is a helper to the bishop with duties less extensive than his and the deacon is the helper of the bishop and presbyter. Even in the New Testament, presbyterate and diaconate appear by divisions and subdivisions of the duties of an initially unique and full ministry: the apostolate.

marry. According to *AC* VIII 47,26 the only clergy who can still marry after their ordination are the lectors and cantors, but no longer the subdeacons. Presbyters, deacons, and subdeacons were not permitted to marry after ordination, but if married they could continue to live regularly in matrimony (II 2,3; VIII 47,5.51).

IV

THE BYZANTINE TRADITION AFTER THE *AC*: DEACONESSES WITHIN THE CLERICAL SYSTEM WITH ORDINATION OF THE SAME KIND AND MEANING AS THE ORDINATION OF THE DEACON, NOTWITHSTANDING THEIR MORE RESTRICTED POWERS—AS THEIR ORDER BECOMES MORE AND MORE SOLELY HONORIFIC—AND THE IMPOSSIBILITY OF THEIR BEING ADMITTED TO THE PRESBYTERATE.

For our topic, the Byzantine tradition after the *AC* is particularly interesting.[66] Here in the Greek tradition the position of the deaconesses, which becomes clearer on many levels as evidenced from the *AC*, reaches its greatest development before its definitive decline between the eleventh and twelfth centuries.

---

[66] The principal documents for our information are: the Council of Chalcedon, the second Council of Trullo from 692, the civil nomocanonical law, historical information, and various epigraphs. According to the surveys done by Kalsbach (pp. 55–56), the documents attest to the diffusion of the institution of the deaconesses after the fourth century for the following Greek Orthodox provinces: Antioch, Syria to Northeast Antioch, Cappadocia, Seleucia to Calycadno, Pontus, Caria, Phrygia and Pisidia, the Hellespont, Armenia Minor (Roman province), Jerusalem (but there, at the end of the sixth century the institute had disappeared). For Byzantium there is ample documentation in ecclesiastical and civil law and in various other historical sources (Kalsbach pp. 64–68). In the Byzantine Church the institution of the deaconesses continued until at least the end of the twelfth century. See Kalsbach p. 65, n. 10. Texts by the canonists T. Balsamon (1140–1195) and M. Blastares from 1335 in Mayer Op. cit. pp. 63–64, 58–59, 65–66. In Theodoros Op. cit. Θεολογία 1954, p. 453, a text by Anna Comnena on the care that her father Alexius I Comnenus (1081–1118) took of the deaconesses. See on p. 580 the rubrics of euchology between the eleventh and fourteenth centuries.

1) Conditions, obligations, tasks of deaconesses and their place among the clergy

Deaconesses could be elected either from the laity—provided that they were virgins or monogamous widows—or from among the constituted virgins, canonical widows, or even from simple nuns or abbesses. In fact, in Byzantine history, the deaconesses were often nuns or abbesses. At least around the eleventh century that was the custom.[67] However, the diaconate of women, as such, was clearly distinct from the aforementioned states of life.

According to the Theodosian Codex of 390,[68] the deaconesses had to be at least sixty years old, in reference to 1 Tim. 5:9. Canon 15 of the Council of Chalcedon in 451 determined that they be no younger than forty.[69] Justinian's *Novella* 6, 6 of 535 said they should be about fifty.[70]

For those who attempted matrimony after their ordination, church law called for excommunication; the civil law of Justinian decreed the death penalty.[71]

According to the general law established by Canon 6 of the Council of Chalcedon,[72] "absolute" ordinations of deaconesses were not permitted; each time they had to be ordained for a

---

[67] See, for example, the rubric of the Parisian *Coisliniano* 213 of the eleventh century (and also of the twelfth or thirteenth century Codex Athenian *Ethn. Bibl. 662*), which introduces the rite for the ordination of deaconesses: "Order for the ordination of the deaconess, who must be at least forty years old, a pure virgin and, according to the practice that is now in force, a clothed nun μονάζουσα μεγαλοσχημῶν). See Theodoros, Θεολογία 1954 p. 580. M. Blastares attests likewise around 1355, referring to ancient texts. See Mayer Op. cit., p. 580. See also Kalsbach Op. cit. pages 54–55; 67–68.

[68] XVI 2,27. See Mayer Op. cit. p. 16. Around the same period Theodore of Mopsuestia rejected this interpretation of 1 Tim. 5:9. See H.B. Swete, *Theodori M. in ep. B. Pauli Com.*, Cambridge 1882 vol. II, pp. 158–159.

[69] See Mayer Op. cit., p. 28.

[70] Ibid. p. 35.

[71] Council of Chalcedon Can. 15 (See Mayer p. 28). Justinian, see Mayer pp. 35–37; 38; 39.

[72] See *Conciliorum Oecumenicorum Decreta* p. 66.

specific church, or *martyrion*, or monastery. From Justinian (527–565) to Heraclius (610–640) the Great Church of Hagia Sophia in Constantinople had forty deaconesses.[73] For their ecclesiastical service (ἐκκλησιαστικὴ ὑπηρεσία), they were financially supported by the respective church.[74]

In Justinian's *Novella* 6, 6 from 535, their tasks were described in this way: "to serve at sacred baptisms and to be present at other secret things, they customarily perform in the venerable mysteries."[75] But what are these "other secret things that they customarily perform in the venerable mysteries"? Much later, the canonist T. Balsamon (1140–1195), attesting that, in his time, there was no longer an ordination of deaconesses, says that when they existed "they [the deaconesses] also had a proper place (βαθμὸν) inside the sanctuary (βῆμα)."[76] Another late author, of the fourteenth century, M. Blastares (c. 1335), reports on the tasks of deaconesses who, according to the opinion of some, when they existed, "were authorized to enter near the holy altar and who, alongside the deacons, performed the tasks of the deacons."[77] However, aside from the responsibility for the baptism of women, the aforementioned statements are not confirmed in the documents.[78]

---

[73] *Novella* 3, 1 of 535 (Mayer Op. cit. pp. 34–35); Fozio, *Syntagma* 30 (Ibid. p. 63).

[74] *Novella* 123, 30 of 546 (Mayer Op. cit. p. 38).

[75] Mayer Op. cit. p. 36.

[76] See Mayer Op. cit. p. 64. The same author adds that, in his time, deaconesses were still ordained (προχειρίζω therefore = order) in Constantinople, but that they did not have access to the βῆμα, but: "In many things they attend to ecclesiastical work (ἐκκλησιάζω) and they direct the gatherings in women's convents."

[77] Mayer Op. cit. p. 66.

[78] In the Byzantine period, one no longer finds mentioned as a duty of deaconesses [the duty] to look after the doors of the church at least to allow women to enter—the duty about which the AC speak and which in Pseudo Ignatius (fourth–fifth centuries; *Ad. Antioch* XII 2: see Mayer Op. cit. p. 33) stands out as a hallmark of deaconesses. Rather, the duty of looking after the doors appears specific to the subdiaconate in the related rite of ordination. See the texts published by J. Morinus, *Commentarius de sacris ecclesiae*

Furthermore, as the baptism of adults gradually ended, the institution of deaconesses also became less common, and where it still continued for some time, it became purely honorific, granted to women of high rank or to nuns and abbesses of monasteries.[79]

Deaconesses, clearly considered part of the clergy along with presbyters, deacons, subdeacons, lectors, and cantors, come right after the deacons in the official lists in which the individual ranks of the clergy are named.[80] It was believed that having received "holy ordination" (τὴν ἱερὰν χειροτονίαν), they constituted a "holy order" (ἱερὰ τάξις) and were part of the ἱερωσύνη.[81] According to the Justianic legislation, among these same clerics, besides deaconesses, the group of ἱερωσύνη always seems to have included only presbyters, deacons, and subdeacons.[82]

---

ordinationibus, second edition, Antwerp 1695 vol. 1 pp. 58, 66, 68, 75, 79. See also J. Goar, *Euchologion*, second edition, Venice 1730, p. 203.

[79] See Kalsbach pp. 68–69.

[80] *Novella* 3.1: Mayer Op. cit. pp. 34–35. In this official list the doorkeepers are also named, but as a group that is clearly distinct from the clergy. See also Kalsbach Op. cit. pp. 67–68.

[81] Justinian's *Novella* 6,6 (Mayer Op. cit. p. 37). In the *Novella* 123, 30 (Mayer p. 36) the ministry of the deaconess is called ἱερὰ διακονία. With regard to the obligation of deaconesses not to marry after ordination, it says "It is a necessity that all of the venerable deaconesses who are ordained (χειροτονεῖν), from the moment of ordination, be cautioned . . . that they, too, must fear God . . . and fear and be ashamed of falling from the holy order (τῆς ἱερᾶς ἐκπεσεῖν τάξεως) knowing that if they ventured to be ashamed of the ordination (*cheirotonia*) or to abandon that holy ordination (τὴν ἱερὰν χειροτονίαν) or to choose, in any case, another, wicked way of life, they will be subject to death . . . If, in fact, in the ancient laws, those who, because of their deceit, were called virgins (= vestal), they were subject to death if they had become corrupted: how much more must we require the same punishment with regard to chastity for those who have true knowledge of God, so that they safeguard what suits nature and respect that which is required for priesthood (τὸ τὲ ὀφειλομένον τῇ ἱεροσύνη τεροῖεν)" (*Novella* 6.6).

[82] According to the lexicon by Lampe, in ancient Christian literature, ἱερωσύνη as it applies to Christians means: 1. the bishops (AC II 34.4; Council of Sardis canon 10); 2. the presbyterate; 3. the major orders in general (Epiphanius, *Expos. fidei* 21 PG 95, 296 A; Theodoret, *Phil.*, I. i. GCS 3, 445;

Consequently, the deaconesses were placed under a special nomocanonical law, as were the clerics.[83]

2) The Byzantine rite for the ordination of deaconesses and its significance in relationship to the other ordinations

This deals with the rite initially established in the Greek Barberini Codex 336 called the "Barberini Euchology," of the eighth century, and then, with some slight variations in the rubrics, from a series of codices up until the fourteenth century.[84]

a) *The rite and the texts.*

> *Prayer for the ordination* (χειροτονία) *of the deaconesses.*
>
> > *When the holy anaphora has ended and the doors (of the sanctuary) have been opened, before the deacon says "remembering all of the saints . . . ," the one who is to be ordained* (ἡ μέλλουσα χειροτονεῖσθαι) *is brought to the pontiff [bishop] who says in a loud*

Pseudo Dionysius *EH* I. i. [PG 3, 372 B]). While, for Epiphanius, the ἱερωσύνη means only bishop, presbyter, deacon, and subdeacon (see above and notes 31–35) and the deaconess is excluded, the Justinian legislation includes the deaconess, but it does not seem to admit lectors and cantors. In fact, if the inability to marry after ordination is required of the ἱερωσύνη, this obligation even according to the canons of the Apostles (*AC* VIII 47.26), did not bind the cantors and lectors. If that is true, only in a later period does the idea that subdeacon and lector are also part of the ἱερωσύνη assert itself within the Byzantine tradition. In the euchology said to be that of Allazio (Morinus Op. cit. I. p. 87 B and Goar p. 197) the lectorate is called: "the first rank within the ἱερωσύνη."

[83] Primarily the quoted regulations of Theodosius and Justinian. See Mayer Op. cit. pp. 15–16; 34–40.

[84] In Morinus Op. cit. the Barberinian texts are transcribed, as well as the *Grottaferrata* codex (*Gb. I* twelfth–thirteenth centuries) and a twelfth-century Vatican codex. (Morinus I pp. 56–57; 65; 80–81). In Theodoros *Θεολογία* 1954 pp. 578–581 there is a review of seven codices. The most interesting for the rubrics is from the Parisian *Coislinian* codex (*Coislin. gr.* 213) from the eleventh century (and the Athenian *Ethn. Bibl.* 662 from the 12th–13th centuries). See also Goar Op. cit. pp. 218–219.

voice "the divine grace . . ." [85] *Meanwhile she bows her head and the pontiff [bishop] places his hand on her head and, making three crosses, says the following prayer:*

O holy and omnipotent God, who have sanctified the woman through the birth in the flesh of your only begotten Son our Lord: you who have given the grace and poured out your Holy Spirit not only to men but also to women: You, even now, O Lord, look upon this servant of yours and call her to the work of your diaconate and send forth in abundance the gift of your Holy Spirit. Keep her in the true faith and may she fulfill everything in her ministry (λειτουργίαν) in an irreprehensible way of life according to your approval because to you, Father, Son and Holy Spirit, are due all glory, honor and adoration, now and forever, world without end. Amen.

And after the Amen, one of the deacons prays in this way:

In peace let us pray to the Lord (*Response*: Kyrie eleison).

For heavenly peace and for the well-being of the whole world, let us pray to the Lord.

For the peace of the whole world, let us pray to the Lord.

For our archbishop N., for his priesthood, for his preservation, peace, health, and salvation and for the work of his hands, let us pray to the Lord.

For N. who is now being made a deaconess (ὑπὲρ τῆς νῦν προχειροζομένης διακονήσσης τῆσδε), [86] for her salvation, let us pray to the Lord.

That the merciful God may grant her an immaculate and irreproachable diaconate, let us pray to the Lord.

---

[85] The complete formula: "The divine grace, which always heals what is weak and replaces what is flawed, promote (προχειρίζεται) [name] to deaconess. Therefore we pray for her, that the grace of the most Holy Spirit might descend upon her."

[86] τῆσδε is missing in Goar's text. See Theodoros *Θεολογία* 1954 p. 576. For the sense of προχειρίζω see above p. 12, n. 9.

For our devout emperor who is loved by God.

So that we may be freed from every danger and need, let us pray to the Lord.

Help us, save us, have pity on us, and guard us with your grace, O God.

While the deacon is saying this prayer, the bishop laying his hand on the hand of she who is to be ordained (τῆς χειροτονουμένης), prays in this way:

Lord and Ruler, who does not reject women who dedicate themselves and who wish to serve properly in your holy dwellings, but receive them in the order of ministers (ἐν τάξει λειτουργῶν): grant your Holy Spirit to this servant of yours who wishes to dedicate herself to you and to fulfill the office (χάρις) of the diaconate, as you granted the grace (χάρις) of the diaconate to Phoebe whom you called to the work of ministry (λειτουργίας). Grant her, O Lord, to persevere without sin in your holy temples, to conduct herself properly, and especially care for her continence and make her perfect as your servant so that even she, when she is before Christ's tribunal, she may receive the just reward for her conduct; for the mercy and the goodness of your only begotten Son through whom you are blessed.

After the response "Amen," the bishop places the diaconal stole (ὠράριον) around her neck, under her veil (μαφόριον), bringing forward the two ends. Then the deacon who stands at the ambo says:

"remembering all the saints, etc."

After the deaconess has received the Body and Blood of Christ, the archbishop gives her the holy chalice; she receives it and places it on the altar.[87]

---

[87] Among the information about the rite for the ordination of deaconesses that might come from non-liturgical sources, that of M. Blastares from about 1335 is interesting. It attests that, according to the ancient codices on the deaconess: "one does everything that one does on the deacons with few

Now let us see what can be learned about the meaning of the ordination of deaconesses from the texts and rites and from the general context for the ordination of other ministers.

b) Cheirotonia *in the ordination of deaconesses as in the other ordinations.* The ordination of deaconesses is called *cheirotonia.* During the two prayers the bishop "places his hand on her head" (ἐπιθέτεσει τὴν χεῖρα, ἔχει τὴν χεῖρα . . .).

A particular tradition in the canonical and didactic documents of the Greek and Byzantine Church explicitly distinguished *cheirotonia* and *cheirothesia*: attributing only to *cheirotonia* what today we call ordination and considering *cheirothesia* as a εὐλογία or blessing.[88]

---

exceptions. She is led to the sacred altar and covered with the veil (μαφορίῳ). And after it has been said: 'Divine grace, which always heals what is weak,' she does not genuflect on either knee, but only bows her head. The pontiff [bishop] places his hand on her head and prays that she might be able to fulfill without fault the work of the deaconess, observing chastity and honesty in her conduct, safeguarding the holy temples; but he does not permit her to serve in the pure mysteries or to handle the *ripidion* (= the small liturgical fan that the deacon is appointed to wave slowly over the chalice after the consecration), as does the deacon. After this the pontiff [bishop] places the deacon's stole (ὠράριον) around her neck, under the veil, bringing it back around across the chest. At the time of Communion, the pontiff shares with her the sacred mysteries, after the deacon. After this she receives the chalice from the hands of the pontiff, however she does not distribute it, but places it right away on the holy altar." (See in Mayer Op. cit. pp. 58–59.)

[88] See the brief documentation of this fact in Vogel, *Chirotonie* . . . pp. 7–12. "The ritual distinction between *cheirotonia* for the orders and *cheirothesia* for subordinate functions of the clerical course of advancement was done gradually only from the eighth century and following and appears clearly only in the juridical documents or of a didactic nature. . . . After Zonaras (c. 1150) and Balsamon (1140–1195)—and despite some hesitation in these two important commentators—*cheirotonia* and *cheirothesia* stabilize: the first term remains reserved for the laying on of hands done by the bishop to the presbyter and deacon; the second indicates the gesture of blessing for the creation of subordinate functionaries. . . . However it suffices to open the liturgical books, especially the Euchology in order to observe that the cultic language did not follow the juridical or didactic diversification

In reality, from the fact that the ordination of deaconesses is called *cheirotonia* and that the gesture that accompanies it is a ἐπίθεσις of the hand, one cannot conclude anything about the nature of such an ordination compared with that of other ministries. According to the texts published by Morinus[89] of the seven ancient euchologies which have in a way more or less the complete series of "ordinations," one can see that: for the bishop, presbyter, deacon, and subdeacon, as well as for the deaconess, the title of the rite is *cheirotonia* and the gesture is ἐπίθεσις of the hand; the same is true for the lector, except that twice in the title προχείρησις is mentioned instead of *cheirotonia*; the "ordination" of the abbot is called προχείρησις (which can mean: promotion) and four out of five times it has the ἐπίθεσις of the hand.

Regarding the title *cheirotonia* and the act of the laying on of the hand, the ordination of the deaconess might be related as much to that of the deacon (presbyter and bishop), as to that of the subdeacon and lector.

The same must be said if one considers the general content of what is asked of God for the ordinand in the ordination: it is always about the gifts of God, of the Holy Spirit, which allow the one being ordained to carry out well the duties of his or her ministry.

From other features, however, the Byzantine ordination of deaconesses is clearly distinguished from that of the subdeacons and lectors—and all the more from that of the other "dignities,"

---

about which we have spoken. The term *cheirotonia* applies as much (in the sequence of the Euchology) to the ordination of the deacon, presbyter, and bishop as much as to the laying on of hands by which means the bursar of a monastery, the lector, cantor, and subdeacon are introduced to their functions. The laying on of hands—whether called *cheirotonia* or *cheirothesia*—is, in the East, part of the ritual for all levels of the hierarchy, even of the subordinates, contrary to the Latin custom." *Ibid.* pp. 10–12.

[89] I. p. 54–102. One notices, however, that the final euchology, by Allazio also noted by Morinus Op. cit., p. 85, seems to represent not the Byzantine tradition, but the Greek Melkite Antiochene and Syrian Churches.

such as that of the archdeacon, abbot, etc.—and is related to that of the deacons, presbyters, and bishops.

c) *Ordination at the foot of the altar* within the sanctuary is obligatory for deaconesses just as it is for the bishop, presbyter, and deacon, and it is prohibited for the subdeacon and lector.

According to the oldest euchology, the eighth-century Barberini Codex (*Codex Barb. gr.* 336), and that of twelfth-thirteenth century *Grottaferrata Gb I*, the ordination of the subdeacon is done in the διακονικόν, that is the sacristy.[90] The later euchologies say that the ordination of the subdeacon is done "either in the diakonikón, or in front of the great doors of the temple."[91] The great doors of the temple seem to be those at the entrance of the church, in the back, facing the altar. According to Goar,[92] the ancient Venetian editions of the euchology say that when a subdeacon is ordained: "the Pontiff [bishop] is on the throne in the exterior vestibule, where he vests for the liturgy." The text of the ordination published by Goar[93] says that in ordaining a subdeacon the pontiff [bishop] "sits by the beautiful door," that is, again it seems, at the entrance door to the nave. With regard to the current custom, I myself have assisted more than once at the ordination of subdeacons done at the *solea* of the central door that leads to the sanctuary, but always outside the sanctuary itself. I would not be able to say whether such is the general custom, nor when it was introduced.

This is how this matter evolved: in the ancient church, at least until the eleventh or twelfth century, the place for ordination of the subdeacon was the sacristy, thus the ordination was semi-private in nature. And then it moved: either into the atrium of the church or inside the church, but in the back next to the en-

[90] Morinus Op. cit. I pp. 74, 79; Goar Op. cit., p. 204.

[91] Coislinian codex of the eleventh century (*Coisl. gr. 213*). See Morinus Op. cit., pp. 68, 74. See also pp. 79, 87.

[92] Goar p. 204.

[93] Goar p. 203. So, too the *Euchologion* (Rome 1873), p. 130.

trance doors, and finally, to the main door of the sanctuary. However, it always remained and still remains carefully outside of the sanctuary.

The same occurred and still occurs for the ordination of the lector or cantor.

From this point of view, Byzantine ordinations are divided into two groups: those that occur at the foot of the altar inside the sanctuary: bishop, presbyter, deacon, deaconess; and those that do not occur at the foot of the altar and are outside the sanctuary: subdeacon, lector, cantor, as well as "ordinations" to other "dignities" (archdeacon, abbot, etc.).

At this point two questions arise: 1) when can one document this distinction; 2) did it have a clear theological significance in the Byzantine ecclesiastical tradition?

Here there is a fundamental and so far as I know unstudied text by Theodore of Mopsuestia (born in Antioch c. 350, and died in Mopsuestia in Cilicia in 428, contemporaneous with the *AC* and with John Chrysostom) that in my opinion can help. With regard to I Tim. 3:8-15, Theodore says:

> It is worth adding that we should not wonder why (Paul) mentions neither subdeacons nor lectors. In fact, they are not grades of the Church (τῶν γὰρ τῇ τῆς ἐκκλησίας λειτουργίᾳ βαθμῶν ἔξωθεν μᾶλλον οὗτοί εἰσῖν): they were created subsequently because of the necessities that were to be fulfilled by other ministers for the good of the many faithful. Therefore the law does not allow them to receive the *cheirotonia* before the altar (ὅθεν οὐδέ νενόμισθαι αὐτοὺς πρὸ τοῦ θυσιαστηρίου τὴν χειροτονίαν δέχεσθαι) because they do not minister to the mystery; rather the lectors do the readings and the subdeacons within [the sanctuary][94] take care of what is needed for the service of the deacons, and also take care of the lighting of the church, because only the presbyters fulfill the

---

[94] The Latin version from the sixth century (see subsequent note) says *"intra diaconicum."*

ministry of the mystery. The first ones fulfill their priestly office, the second ones minister to the sacred things.[95]

From this text one can see that the theory that is later defended by Simeon of Thessalonica[96]—aside from his terminology, which opposes *cheirotonia* and *cheirothesia*—through which he distinguishes between two groups of ordinations based on those that take place at the foot of the altar in the sanctuary or those that are done outside the sanctuary: this has deep, solemn roots in the Greek liturgical and didactic tradition, which attached to that distinction a precise theological concept.

Theodore of Mopsuestia is very familiar with deaconesses and appreciates them as an apostolic institution, as did John Chrysostom and Theodoret of Cyrrhus[97] around the same period, and as the Byzantine ordination rite presumes when it calls to mind

---

[95] *Theodori episcopi mopsuestiani in ep. B. Pauli Commentarii,* ed. H. B. Swete, University Press, Cambridge 1882, vol. 2, pp. 132–134. The text is preserved in its whole in an African Latin version from the sixth century. Until the mark + it also has the Greek text from the series of excerpts. The Latin text was noted in the East in the ninth century. Rabanus Maurus cites it (*Enar. In ep. Pauli,* lib. 23 *In ep. I ad Tim* cap. 3 PL 112, 607 C–D) and also Amalarius who attributes it to Ambrose, *Liber officialis* II 6 n.2 (ed Hanssens II 213–214). Note: the same practice, around the same period, seems to be confirmed by a passage from the Council *ad Quercum* from 403, in which, among the other accusations made against John Chrysostom, the thirteenth was: that "he had ordained presbyters and deacons without being at the altar" (See Hefele-Leclercq, *Hist. des conc.* II/I p. 144). It says nothing about the ordinations of lectors and subdeacons, probably, indeed, because these were not done at the altar.

[96] *De sacr. ord.* Op. cit. 156 PG 155, 361–363. "There are two ordinations outside of the βῆμα, those of the lector and subdeacon. There are others, as well: those of the officials, the delegate or the candle-bearer. . . . However, the noble ordinations (ἐξαίρετοι = main, chief, most important) are done inside the βῆμα."

[97] For Theodore of Mopsuestia: *In I Tim* 3:11 (ed. Swete II, pp. 128–129; 158–159). For John Chrysostom, *Hom. In. ep. ad Rom* 30:2 PG 60,663 C–664 A; In *I Tim II,* I PG 62, 553 D. For Theodoret of Cyrus: *In I Tim.* 3:1 PG 82, 809 A; *In Rom* 16:1–2: Phoebe PG 82, 217 D.

Phoebe. However, these authors do not provide details about how and where the ordinations of deaconesses were done, nor do they compare them to the ordinations of the subdeacon and lector.

Nevertheless, it is true that the Byzantine tradition, as attested by the euchologies distinguishing between the ordinations that are done in the sanctuary and those that are done outside, and placing the ordination of deaconesses in the first group, equates that ordination with that of the deacon, even though the deaconesses' powers are more restricted, and they are not allowed to serve at the altar during the celebration of the Mass.

d) *The moment of the ordination of deaconesses,* when it occurs within the Mass,[98] is at the end of the anaphora before the prayers in preparation for the distribution of Communion. That is precisely the moment at which the ordination of the deacon also occurs. The subdeacon is ordained in the first part, the didactic part of the Mass. Even here one can see that the ordination of deaconesses is comparable to that of the deacons and not to that of the subdeacons.

e) *The formula: "the divine grace. . . ."* The structure of the prayers said over the deaconess during her ordination is wholly the same as that of the deacon: the initial formula included *the divine grace. . . .* In the Byzantine rite this formula, in contrast with what occurs in the Syriac tradition, is used only in the ordination of the bishop, presbyter, and deacon, but not in that of the subdeacons or other ministers or officials.

This is an additional serious argument which indicates that the ordination of deaconesses in the Byzantine tradition was considered to be of the same nature and significance as that of the deacons, presbyters, and bishops, and that it was not

---

[98] According to a rubric from the codex *Barberini gr. 336* (see Morinus Op. cit., I p. 80 C–D) the ordination of deaconesses, as with that of the deacons, can also occur in the so-called Mass of the Presanctified, and so it is done before Communion.

comparable to that of the subdeacon, nor was it considered a simple benediction.

In fact, recent studies[99] have demonstrated, above all, the antiquity of the formula, also confirming the assertions made by Simeon of Thessalonica. The fact that it is used in a nearly identical way within all of the Eastern rites makes one presume that it already existed before the separations, particularly before 431, since the formula is also used by the Nestorians. Secondly, these studies have demonstrated the importance of the formula in the Eastern rites in the way they conceptualize ordination itself. According to later Latin models, one should probably say that, for the Eastern Churches, the formula "the divine grace . . ." was, at least originally, an indispensable part of the basic formula of the sacrament, along with the two epicletic prayers that usually follow. Therefore, the fact that, in the Byzantine tradition, such a formula is not used for the subdeacon and for the lector is a further argument to say that that tradition considered the ordination of the subdeacon and lector to be of a different nature and to have a different significance than the ordination of the deaconess and deacon.

f) *The diaconal orarion is* given to the deaconess by the bishop at the end of her ordination rite. But the deaconess wore a veil that covered her head and also her shoulders: the μαφόριον.[100] The diaconal stole was placed around her neck, under the veil, in a way that the two ends hung in front of her chest—the deacon, on the other hand, wore the stole on the left shoulder in a way that the one end hung in front and the other in back. This feature also relates the deaconess to the deacon, because the diaconal stole is the sign, *par excellence*, of the deacon and his

---

[99] J. M. Hanssens, *La forme sacramentelle dans les ordinations sacerdotales du rit grec*, in *Gregorianum* 5 (1924) 208–227; 6 (1925) 41–80. B. Botte, *La formule d'ordination: "La grâce divine" dans les rites orientaux*, in *L'Orient syrien* 2 (1957) 285–296. E. Lanne, *Les ordinations dans le rite copte, Ibid.* 5 (1960) 81–106.

[100] See Morinus Op. cit. I p. 179 n. 14.

ministry. Even long ago ecclesiastical law explicitly prohibited subdeacons, lectors, and cantors to wear the orarion, the specific sign of the diaconal ministry.[101]

g) *The chalice.* After ordination the deaconess received Communion right after the deacons.[102] There is no reason to doubt that she received Communion in the same way as the deacons: inside the sanctuary, first receiving the host from the bishop in her hands, and then drinking from the chalice that he offered her. After this, as also occurred with the deacon, she received the same chalice from the hands of the bishop. The difference, however, was that the deacon received the chalice in order then to distribute it to the communicants outside of the sanctuary, at the entrance of the holy door: the deaconess, instead, once she received the chalice went to place it on the altar.

This is an ambiguous act, as part of a compromise to indicate a status above that of the subdeacon (who always received Communion outside of the sanctuary and without the ability to hold the chalice with the blood), but not equal to the status of the deacons: even if apparently more akin to the status of the deacon than of the subdeacon.

With the aforementioned gesture of the chalice, the Byzantine tradition hints somewhat at the idea, without bringing it neatly to a conclusion, that in later Latin models, one could name as a certain *potestas* of the deaconess *in eucharistiam.* It is noteworthy that the Nestorian and Monophysite traditions largely carried this concept forward since the fifth-sixth centuries, clearly granting the deaconesses also the power to distribute Communion to

---

[101] Council of Laodicea, canons 22 and 23 transmitted to the *Corpus Juris* dist. 23 chapters 27 and 28. See, for example, Hefele-Leclercq, *Hist. des conc.* I/2 p. 1012.

[102] See explicitly codex *Coisl.* gr. 213. See Theodoros, Θεολογία 1954, p. 580 (see also 581), and also M. Blastarès: cited above p. 179 n. 1.

women and children in certain circumstances, in the absence of the presbyter or deacon.[103]

CONCLUSION

In conclusion, for our purpose we must first of all observe that in Christian antiquity there were different beliefs and tendencies distinguishing between ministry and ministry, ordination and ordination, with regard to the nature and significance of the respective orders or ranks.

1. *The Apostolic Tradition* of Hippolytus (c. 210) is the first extant document that talks about the way in which bishops, presbyters, deacons, widows, lectors, virgins, and subdeacons were established—it ignores deaconesses—and their respective tasks as well as their *raison d'être* in the church. Now, with regard to the meaning and ways in which each of these were constituted, Hippolytus in the *Tradition* makes a clear distinction between two groups of male ministers: bishops, presbyters, and deacons on one side, lectors and subdeacons, on the other, while widows and virgins appear there as ways of life and not as ministries. From the point of view of ritual, for Hippolytus, the difference between these two groups is that only the bishops, presbyters, and deacons receive the laying on of hands while he asserts persistently that the lector (n. 11) and the subdeacon (n. 13) cannot receive it. In n. 10 of the text edited by Botte,[104] after having said that one must not lay hands on the widow because "she does not offer the oblation" (προσφορά) and does not have the λειτουργία," he adds as a general principal: *"cheirotonia* is given only to the cleric (χλῆρος) in view of the λειτουργία." The λειτουργία here seems to mean the service focused on the altar, which the

---

[103] See the texts in Mayer, Op. cit. p. 33 lines 2–3 (*Testamentum Domini*); p. 52, 22–25 (Severus of Antioch, c. 465–538); p. 53, 2–3; 3–7 (John of Tella, c. 483–538); p. 54, 2–3 (James of Edessa, d. 578).

[104] Pp. 30–31.

bishop, presbyter, and deacon perform and the lector and sub-deacon cannot perform.

The Western tradition after Hippolytus always not only makes a distinction, like Hippolytus, between two groups—bishop, presbyter, deacon and lector, subdeacon—but besides, and always, as with Hippolytus, it makes the aforementioned distinction on the ritual basis of the presence or absence of the laying on of hands. This, at least until the time when, in the West, the opinion spread that also in the constitution of the bishop, the presbyter, and the deacon the *traditio instrumentorum* or the anointing, respectively, played a role.

2. On the other hand, in the Eastern tradition, ordination was not only conferred on the bishop, presbyter, deacon, and deacon-ess, but also on the lector and subdeacon. In the Antiochene tradition, it is even used for the installation of "offices" ὀφριχία, as with the bursar and the archdeacon, for the head of the mon-astery, etc. In this tradition, therefore, the distinction between the "orders" is not made on the basis of the laying on of hands. In the tradition of the Byzantine euchologies, a distinction be-tween *cheirotonia* and *cheirothesia*, which appears in the eighth century and following, is not even understood by many authors. It stabilizes only after about the middle of the twelfth century, as if it were only the presbyter and deacon ordained by *cheiro-tonia*, whereas the ministers who were inferior to them would be ordained by *cheirothesia*, the equivalent of what today we call a simple blessing.[105]

Nonetheless, the ancient Greek tradition sometimes sought to establish, and did establish in another way, a distinction among groups of ministers on the list: bishop, presbyter, deacon, deaconess, lector, subdeacon.

3. Epiphanius of Salamis[106] distinguished the ministers who belong to the ἱερωσύνη: bishops, presbyters, deacons, subdeacons,

---

[105] See above, pp. 48–50.
[106] See above, para. II n. 2.

and those who do not belong to it and only come *after* the ἱερωσύνη: lectors, deaconesses, exorcists, interpreters, undertakers, and doorkeepers. However, one cannot know with certainty what Epiphanius meant by ἱερωσύνη, or why, for example, the subdeacon belongs to it but neither does the deaconess nor the lector.

4. Theodore of Mopsuestia[107] is a witness to an ecclesiastical law that does not allow either lectors or subdeacons, and much less other offices, to be ordained at the foot of the altar inside the sanctuary, and infers that the reason for this is that "they were established subsequently" and "they do not minister the same mystery"; therefore "they are instead outside of the ranks of Church ministry." With this, Theodore is a witness to the theological thinking that there exists a distinction between the bishop, presbyter, deacon group on one side, and the lector, subdeacon group on the other, and that such a distinction has a ritual expression in the fact that the first ones are ordained at the foot of the altar inside the sanctuary and the second ones are not. Theodore does not talk about deaconesses in this context, though he is familiar with them and understands them to be an apostolic institution. One might also suppose that the *Apostolic Constitutions* (same region, Syria, and the same period as Theodore), speaking with great clarity about the ordination of deaconesses and saying that this occurs in the presence of the presbytery, the deacons, and deaconesses (VIII 19,2), presumes with this that it occurs in public, and presumably in front of the altar in the sanctuary, as opposed to ordination of the subdeacons and lectors (VIII 21.22), which took place in the διακονικόν.[108] Later, Simeon of Thessalonica affirmed the principle: "noble (or principal) ordinations are done inside the βῆμα."[109]

---

[107] See above, pp. 51–53.
[108] See above, para. III n. 5 b.
[109] See above, p. 53.

5. From the moment that one documents the Byzantine tradition of euchologies (seventh-eighth centuries) and until the pertinent rites were transcribed in those texts (fourteenth century), deaconesses always appear to have been ordained at the foot of the altar inside the sanctuary in clear and deliberate juxtaposition to what was done in the ordination of lectors, subdeacons, or other "offices." Other ritual details for the Byzantine ordination of deaconesses go along the same lines: the moment of ordination, the use of the formula "the divine grace . . .", the orarion, Communion after the deacons from the hands of the bishop in the sanctuary, the fact of receiving from the bishop the chalice that the deaconess then went to place on the altar.

With all of this, it seems to me certain that in the history of the undivided church the Byzantine tradition maintained that by nature and dignity the ordination of deaconesses belonged to the group of bishops, presbyters, and deacons and not to the group of lectors and subdeacons, and even less to that of the other offices or dignities that came to be established ritually outside of the sanctuary.

6. If one accepts what has been said thus far, one must also acknowledge the following conclusion: theologically, in virtue of the use of the Byzantine Church, it appears that women can receive diaconal ordination, which, by nature and dignity, is equated to the ordination of the deacons, and not simply to that of the subdeacons or lectors, and much less, to use the terminology of today, to that of some lesser ministry constituted by what today one would call a simple benediction.

7. It is nevertheless true that in the same Byzantine tradition the liturgical work of the deaconesses was far more restricted than that of the male deacons. But it is also true that, in the same custom of the church today, from this perspective, the situation is already largely obsolete with regard to the distribution of Communion and many other tasks. It is noteworthy that today there are cases in which, by indult, women do almost everything that can be done by the clergy, except say Mass, hear confessions,

and do the anointing of the sick.[110] It is also true that the ancient tradition of the church unanimously denied women the pos-

[110] The fact of not having granted women the permission to do anointing of the sick is connected to the Western scholastic and later idea that sees such anointing as above all a type of supplement to penance for the remission of sins. This fact excessively relegates to secondary status the idea of the rite as a means of obtaining from God healing from illness, an idea that, rather, is primary in many ancient sources. However, in the ancient Eastern tradition it appears more than once that among the duties of the deaconess, providing anointing of the sick to women was included. There is no historical basis on which to interpret this anointing without doubt to a sacramental in the modern sense, as opposed to a sacrament. As is often repeated, such a distinction in both the East and Latin West before scholasticism was anything but clear. Among the historically documented ways to anoint the sick in the Greek tradition the most ancient seems to be that of anointing the whole body, in particular, the parts that are ill (testimony of Theodulf in the eighth-century ms. of Sinai 960, from the thirteenth century: see J. Dauvillier, *Extrême Onction dans les Eglises orientales*, in *Dict. De Droit Can.* V (1953) 731–733). The general custom explained by Epiphanius (*Haer.* 79.3 PG 62, 744 D–745A) was that every time one had to expose a woman's body in the rite, the deaconess intervened for reasons of propriety. See also J. Danielou, *Le ministère des femmes dans l'èglise ancienne*, in: *La Maison-Dieu* 61 (1960) 94. For the Syrian Monophysite Church there is the testimony of James of Edessa (d. 578): see Mayer Op. cit., pp. 53–54; of Bar Hebraeus (1226–1286): see W. De Vries, *Sakramententheologie bei den syrischen Monophysiten*, Rome 1940 p. 220. The Maronite tradition is summarized by the Lebanese synod of 1736, specifically approved by Benedict XIV in 1741. Of the deaconesses: "officia sunt, ut muliebri hoestati ac pudore in ecclesia consulatur . . . 3. ut chrismate vel oleo nuda earum corpora tam in baptismo et confirmatione, *quam in extrema unction ungant*, defunctas etiam lavent et sepeliant . . . Quamvis autem diaconissarum officia, quoad sacramenta baptismi, confirmationis et extremae unctionis jam diu cessarint, quum non amplius totius corporis unctiones fiant: durant tamen quoad dicatas Deo in sacris coenobiis virgines, quibus abatissae praeficiuntur. Abatissae enim diaconissarum benedictionem accipiunt, et munia omnia quae illis in conciliis sunt concessa exequuntur." Mansi 38 col. 163–164. Moreover, it is the case historically that in the ancient church the faithful often provided themselves with the anointing of the sick with the oil blessed by the priest for this purpose. Again, this does not demonstrate that it was considered only a "sacramental." See Dauvillier Op. cit., 725–789.

sibility of entering the priesthood. Such was affirmed with different arguments, the value of which it is the place of theology to reflect on at each occasion.

S. Anselmo, Rome
Cipriano Vaggagini, O.S.B.

Contributors

Carmela Leonforte-Plimack has been a teacher of English in Rome for twenty years and is a research assistant in the Department of Religion at Hofstra University, Hempstead, N.Y. She holds the Ph.D. in religious history from "*La Sapienza*," the University of Rome.

Amanda Quantz is associate professor of theology and director of the pastoral ministry program at the University of Saint Mary, Leavenworth, Kansas. An historical theologian, she specializes in Medieval Christianity and the Eastern Churches. She earned her Ph.D. at the University of St. Michael's College, Toronto.

Phyllis Zagano is senior research associate-in-residence and adjunct professor of religion at Hofstra University, Hempstead, N.Y. She has published widely on the restoration of women to the ordained diaconate. Her Ph.D. is from the State University of New York at Stony Brook.